1974

THE DECLARATION OF INDEPENDENCE
And What It Means Today

THE
DECLARATION
OF INDEPENDENCE
And What It Means Today

BY

EDWARD DUMBAULD

NORMAN

UNIVERSITY OF OKLAHOMA PRESS

By Edward Dumbauld

Interim Measures of Protection in International Controversies
(The Hague, 1932)

Thomas Jefferson, American Tourist
(Norman, 1946)

The Declaration of Independence and What It Means Today
(Norman, 1950)

The Political Writings of Thomas Jefferson
(New York, 1955)

The Bill of Rights and What It Means Today
(Norman, 1957)

The Constitution of the United States
(Norman, 1964)

COPYRIGHT 1950 BY THE UNIVERSITY OF OKLAHOMA PRESS
PUBLISHING DIVISION OF THE UNIVERSITY
MANUFACTURED IN THE U.S.A.
FIRST EDITION, AUGUST, 1950
SECOND PRINTING, APRIL, 1968

To M. W. D.

*Comme l'étendard de la Pucelle, elle avait été à la peine,
c'était bien raison qu'elle fût à l'honneur.*

PREFACE

On the Fourth of July each year, the heart of every American is stirred anew as he rereads the Declaration of Independence. Its perennial appeal is primarily due to the philosophy of government which it expresses, and which Americans heartily endorse: that is to say, the philosophy which recognizes government as a man-made device for promoting human welfare, an instrumentality which the people may remodel or replace whenever it fails to give satisfactory service.

This is a political principle of universal validity. It did not exhaust its vitality when George III was ousted as ruler of thirteen small states in America. It is applicable today, and anywhere. If the Japanese understood the Declaration of Independence, they would know that neither the "son of heaven" nor the son of Arthur MacArthur had any divine right to rule over them. If the people of the whole world understood the Declaration of Independence, they would know that they could replace obsolete nationalistic machinery of government by such newly instituted form of world-wide government as should seem to them most likely to effect their safety and happiness.

Like Jefferson, all Americans know, and will therefore say, that the state is the servant, not the master, of the people; that it is a machine established for their use, hence subject to their superintendence and control; that it is a means, not an end; that it is a human contrivance, not a divine entity superior to its citizens, which they must worship and adore, before which they must bow down and sacrifice. In America the state is merely a useful political mechanism employed by the people to transact their public business. It is not a mystical, glorified, metaphysical monstrosity as in nations where totalitarian collectivism and similar dogmas prevail.

But to understand fully the Declaration of Independence, it

is necessary to do more than merely endorse the political philosophy which it propounds. One must be familiar with its historical background, with ideas and events which are now forgotten but were in the forefront of men's minds at the time it was written. One must know something of the political and constitutional standards and customs that were cherished in those days, and of the grievances which filled with dismay the hearts of our forefathers.

Undoubtedly there have been many Americans reading the Declaration who have shared my desire to understand it better, to interpret it correctly, to grasp its full meaning, and to ponder its significance for us today.

But such study of this famous state paper has been difficult because no convenient commentary on the Declaration was available. Professor Edward S. Corwin's *The Constitution and What It Means Today* exemplifies the type of treatment which the Declaration of Independence, an equally important document in our nation's history, deserves, but has never hitherto received.

The present volume is thus designed for the accommodation of readers desiring to ascertain the meaning of any particular passage of the text of the Declaration. Accordingly, I have sought to present relevant data in convenient form, rather than to develop a significantly original treatment of the subject. I have included in my commentary, however, any observations that seemed pertinent and interesting, whether novel or otherwise. In connection with many passages in the Declaration, I have referred to related ideas appearing elsewhere in Jefferson's writings or in sources he may have used.

In the Introduction, I have discussed briefly the adoption of the Declaration and the texts of the Declaration. These subjects are treated at length in the works of Hazelton, Friedenwald, Becker, and Boyd, of which the last-named is especially helpful because the manuscripts in Jefferson's handwriting are photographically reproduced. Every change made in the course of drafting the Declaration is there enumerated, and the evolution of the text can be visually studied by the reader. Since this most useful work is readily available, I have, in connection with each particular passage of the text of the Declaration, included a reference to changes made during the course of its drafting only where the meaning was affected by such alterations. Mere modifications in verbiage and style have been disregarded, as well as the peculiarities of Jefferson's spelling and capitalization.

Thomas Jefferson considered his authorship of the Declaration of Independence foremost among the achievements for which he wished to be remembered by posterity. This verdict will be confirmed by anyone who today studies this immortal document and its contribution to the development of those political traditions which Jefferson called "Americanism." In his old age, when almost half a century had passed since the Declaration of Independence was given to the world, its author spoke of it with earnest reverence in words which all who now love freedom may most fittingly repeat: "I pray God that these principles may be eternal."

Edward Dumbauld

Washington, D. C.
April 13, 1950

CONTENTS

ILLUSTRATIONS

THE DECLARATION OF INDEPENDENCE

And What It Means Today

INTRODUCTION
Adoption of the Declaration

WHEN the Continental Congress at Philadelphia on the Fourth of July, 1776, adopted the Declaration of Independence, it marked the end of British authority over the American Colonies. The drastic and irrevocable step of thus proclaiming complete separation from the mother country was not taken hastily or inadvisedly. It came as the culmination of a long series of events, which convinced Americans that their freedom and happiness were unattainable under British rule. It demonstrated dramatically the truth of Edmund Burke's dictum that "a great empire and little minds go ill together." For the sake of an abstract dogma of political theory, the narrow-minded government in London lost a continent.

The discord between the Colonies and the home government began soon after George III became king in 1760. In 1761 public opinion in America was aroused against England by the eloquent argument of James Otis in opposition to use of the odious "writs of assistance" as a means of repressing smuggling in Massachusetts. Otis declared that an act of Parliament contrary to natural right was unconstitutional and void.[1]

In 1763 the end of the Seven Years' War eliminated the menace of French power in America. But in that same year a proclamation was made by George III on October 7, 1763, prohibiting settlement west of the Ohio River. In opposing westward expansion, the British government sought to thwart one of the strongest forces in American life. The defeat of France, removing the fear of danger from a hostile neighbor, lessened the Colonists' feeling of need for British protection, while their own

[1] John Adams, in contemporary memoranda and subsequently elaborated reminiscences, recorded for posterity Otis's argument in *Paxton's Case. Works*, II, 521–25; X, 314–62. For an account of this case, see also Samuel M. Quincy (ed.), *Reports of Cases . . . By Josiah Quincy, Junior*, 51–57.

military exploits during the course of the war heightened their sense of confident self-reliance. At the same time, the expenses incurred for defense of American possessions began to bear heavily upon the British government, and resulted in attempts to raise a revenue by taxing the Colonies.

To relieve the burdens under which taxpayers in England groaned, the cabinet of George Grenville passed the Stamp Act of March 22, 1765.[2] This legislation provoked a storm of opposition in America. The Colonies sent delegates to a congress which met at New York and adopted resolutions on October 19, 1765, declaring that such an imposition was unconstitutional and petitioning for its repeal. Similar sentiments had been voiced in Virginia, as a result of the bold and compelling eloquence of Patrick Henry in the House of Burgesses.[3] Although only nine colonies were represented in the Stamp Act Congress, that body was a precursor of the Continental Congress which met in 1774 and succeeding years, constituting the first federal government in the United States.

On March 18, 1766, the Stamp Act was repealed on the ground that its continuance "would be attended with many inconveniencies, and may be productive of consequences greatly detrimental to the commercial interests of these kingdoms." At the same time, however, Parliament passed a Declaratory Act, in which it asserted its unlimited power to legislate for America in all cases whatsoever.

The act proclaimed:

> That the said colonies and plantations in America have been, are, and of right ought to be, subordinate unto, and dependent upon the imperial crown and parliament of Great Britain; and that the King's majesty, by and with the advice and consent of the lords spiritual and temporal, and commons of Great Britain, in parliament assembled, had, hath, and of right ought to have, full

[2] For citations of acts of Parliament, see Bibliography, page 171.

[3] For the Virginia resolves of May 30, 1765, and accounts of Henry's speech, see *Journals of the House of Burgesses of Virginia 1761–1765*, 360; Samuel E. Morison, *Sources and Documents illustrating the American Revolution*, 14–18. Jefferson, then a law student, heard Henry speak, and thought the orator's eloquence comparable to Homer. Edward Dumbauld, *Thomas Jefferson, American Tourist*, 33.

power and authority to make laws and statutes of sufficient force and validity to bind the colonies and people of America, subjects of the crown of Great Britain, in all cases whatsoever.

A second section of the act declared null and void all Colonial resolutions, votes, orders, and proceedings denying or drawing into question the powers of Parliament.

The unbounded authority thus claimed, Parliament proceeded to exercise by enacting legislation, sponsored by Chancellor of the Exchequer Charles Townshend, imposing a duty on glass, lead, paper, tea, and other articles. Later the tax was repealed, except upon the importation of tea. Townshend imagined that he had cleverly outwitted the colonists by adopting taxes which were "external," and therefore within the power of Parliament under the theory accepted by William Pitt and by many American political thinkers which distinguished between external and internal taxes. Townshend himself regarded the distinction as "perfect nonsense."

This theory recognized Parliament as the supreme imperial legislature, but distinguished between ordinary legislation and tax laws. With respect to the former, each branch of Parliament is merely co-ordinate with the king (the true legislator in the British state, strictly speaking, being the "king in Parliament"). But with respect to the latter, the House of Commons alone has authority to act for the property owners represented in that body in making a grant or gift of a portion of their property to the king for the support of his government. Since American property owners were not represented in Parliament, and since a grant of their property could be made only by their own representatives, it followed that their property could not be granted away by Parliament, and that any attempt by Parliament to tax the Colonies would be equivalent to an unauthorized gift of one person's property by an agent representing someone else.

Benjamin Franklin, in his examination at the bar of the House of Commons on February 13, 1766, had stressed the distinction between internal and external taxation, but admitted that no such distinction was expressed in the words of the Colonial charters. When asked whether the colonists might not object also to Parliament's right of external taxation, he replied: "They never have hitherto. Many arguments have been lately used here to shew them that there is no difference, and that if you have no right to tax them internally, you have no right to tax them externally, or make any other law to bind them. At present they do not reason so, but in time they may possibly be convinced by these arguments." Prominent among the extremists denying the possibility of any valid distinction or tenable middle ground was Lord Mansfield, who contended that "the supremacy of the British legislature must be complete, entire, and unconditional; or on the other hand, the colonies must be free and independent."[4]

Townshend's legislation alarmed John Dickinson, the conservative Philadelphia statesman, who published in 1767 his *Letters from a Farmer* to warn his apathetic countrymen against acquiescence in an exercise of power which he feared was as dangerous as the more popularly noticed Stamp Act.[5] Dickinson distinguished between the power to tax, which he claimed exclusively for American governments, and the power to regulate commerce, which he recognized as belonging to Parliament.[6] He considered as a tax the expense of complying with a requirement imposed by law, such as furnishing supplies for the army. He likewise regarded as a tax the imposition of a duty on the exportation to the Colonies alone of any article of necessity which they were forbidden to obtain except from England.[7] Dickinson's distinction proved to be as fruitless as the earlier distinction between external and internal taxes. The Townshend Acts had the effect of demonstrating that any Parliamentary taxation whatever would be unacceptable to the colonists. Americans soon aban-

[4] *The Parliamentary History of England, from the Earliest Period to the Year 1803*, XVI, 144, 158-59 (hereafter cited as *Parliamentary History*). For Lord Mansfield's statement, see *ibid.*, XVIII, 269. For Lord Camden's declaration that taxation without representation is robbery, and Chatham's distinction between taxation and legislation, see *ibid.*, XVI, 177-78; XVIII, 165-66. On the earlier history of the property theory of taxation, see also John Rushworth, *Historical Collections*, I, 513; IV, 34.

[5] *Letters from a Farmer in Pennsylvania, To the Inhabitants of the British Colonies*, 7, 13. The *Letters* appeared in newspapers before publication in pamphlet and book form, the first letter being dated November 4, 1767.

[6] *Ibid.*, 13-16.

[7] *Ibid.*, 8, 19-20.

doned "the half-way house of John Dickinson," and reached the conclusion that Parliament had no legislative power at all over the Colonies.[8]

Thus the matter stood, a mere theoretical difference without serious political consequences, until British troops were sent to Massachusetts in 1768. This display of military force fomented antagonism. Events such as the Boston Massacre of March 5, 1770, and the Tea Party of December 16, 1773, then led Parliament to pass in 1774 the five "Intolerable Acts." Of these, the first was the Boston Port Act, which cut off all the commerce of that city. Another act reorganized the government of Massachusetts, so as to lessen the influence of the people and increase the powers of the crown. A third act provided that trials for murder committed in the course of suppressing riots or enforcing the revenue laws might be transferred to England or to another colony, if the royal governor felt that an impartial trial could not be had in Massachusetts. An amended Quartering Act made the colony chargeable for the support of English troops at the place where they were stationed, even if barracks were already available in the vicinity. The Quebec Act, "extending the boundaries, and changing the Government and Religion of" that province, "erected . . . a tyranny dangerous to the very existence of all" the English-speaking colonies whose opportunities for western migration were curtailed.[9]

Again America was aroused, as in the days of the Stamp Act, and a Continental Congress convened in Philadelphia at Carpenter's Hall on September 5, 1774. It sat until October 26, 1774. A committee was promptly appointed to state "the rights of the Colonies in general, the several instances in which these rights are violated or infringed, and the means most proper to be pursued for obtaining a restoration of them." A report dealing with rights was brought in on September 22, 1774, and two days later one regarding infringements and violations. On September 24, 1774, it was resolved "That the congress do confine themselves,

[8] Thomas Jefferson, *Works*, I, 14; II, 71; V, 187–89; James Madison, *Writings*, VIII, 414. Cf. John Quincy Adams, *Memoirs*, VIII, 279, 284; Edmund S. Morgan, "Colonial Ideas of Parliamentary Power," *The William and Mary Quarterly* (3rd series), Vol. V, No. 3 (July, 1948), 325–26, 330, 340.

[9] Jefferson, *Works*, II, 103, 117.

at present, to the consideration of such rights only as have been infringed by acts of the British parliament since the year 1763, postponing the further consideration of the general state of American rights to a future day."

After considerable discussion, the Congress adopted on October 14, 1774, a set of ten resolutions embodying a declaration of the political rights claimed by the Colonies. Their demand was placed upon a threefold foundation: the "natural rights" of mankind, the traditional constitutional rights of Englishmen, and the specific rights granted by Colonial charters.[10]

In these resolutions, the Americans, relying upon "the immutable laws of nature, the principles of the English constitution, and the several charters or compacts," declared "That they are entitled to life, liberty, & property, and they have never ceded to any sovereign power whatever, a right to dispose of either without their consent." Their ancestors were "entitled to all the rights, liberties and immunities of free and natural-born subjects, within the realm of England," and by their emigration to America "they by no means forfeited, surrendered, or lost any of those rights." The fourth resolution proclaimed "That the foundation of English liberty, and of all free government, is a right in the people to participate in their legislative council." Since the colonists cannot properly be represented in the British Parliament, their own local legislatures are entitled to exclusive power of legislation, subject to the traditional royal veto. "But, from the necessity of the case, and a regard to the mutual interest of both countries, we cheerfully consent to the operation of such acts of the British parliament" as are limited to bona fide regulation of external commerce, "excluding every idea of taxation, internal or external, for raising a revenue on the subjects in America, without their consent." This wording was a compromise drafted by John Adams, after lengthy debate among those who differed in opinion about the degree of power which should be recognized as belonging to Parliament.

[10] *Journals of the Continental Congress* (edited by Worthington C. Ford), I, 63–73 (hereafter cited as *Journals*); John Adams, *Works*, II, 370–77. John Dickinson did not take his seat in Congress until three days after the adoption of these resolutions.

The resolutions went on to claim for the Colonies the benefit of the common law, especially trial by a jury "of the vicinage," as well as of English statutes applicable to their local circumstances, and of the immunities and privileges granted and confirmed by royal charters or secured by the codes of provincial laws.

It was also declared illegal to keep a standing army in time of peace without the consent of the legislature, or to interfere with the right of the people peaceably to assemble and petition for redress of grievances.

In conclusion, the resolutions asserted the principle of separation of powers. "It is indispensably necessary to good government, and rendered essential by the English constitution, that the constituent branches of the legislature be independent of each other; that, therefore, the exercise of legislative power in several colonies, by a council appointed, during pleasure, by the crown, is unconstitutional, dangerous, and destructive to the freedom of American legislation."

After proceeding to specify violations of the foregoing rights which had occurred since the end of the Seven Years' War in 1763, the Congress resolved for the time being to adopt only three "peaceable measures" for obtaining redress: to curtail trade with Great Britain by entering into an "association" or agreement for that purpose; to prepare an address to the people of Great Britain, as well as a memorial to the inhabitants of British America; and to prepare a loyal address to the King.[11]

Other noteworthy action taken by the first Continental Congress included a resolution of October 8, 1774, approving the opposition by Massachusetts "to the execution of the late acts of Parliament; and if the same shall be attempted to be carryed [sic] into opposition by force, in such case all America ought to support them in their opposition," and a resolution of October 21, 1774, "That the seizing, or attempting to seize any person in America, in order to transport such person beyond the sea, for trial of offences, committed within the body of a county in Amer-

11 The first of these measures was adopted on October 18, 1774; the second on October 21, 1774; the third on October 26, 1774. *Journals*, I, 75–81, 81–101, 115–21.

ica, being against law, will justify, and ought to meet with resistance and reprisal."[12]

But though the Congress strongly protested against violations of rights claimed for the American Colonies, no demand for independence was put forward in 1774. The same was true in 1775, when the second Continental Congress met at the State House in Philadelphia on May 10, 1775, and sat until August 2, 1775. Indeed, the future author of the Declaration, as late as August 25, 1775, made the statement: "I am sincerely one of those [who still wish for re-union with their parent country], and would rather be in dependence on Great Britain, properly limited, than on any other nation on earth, or than on no nation. But I am one of those, too, who, rather than submit to the rights of legislating for us, assumed by the British Parliament, and which late experience has shown they will so cruelly exercise, would lend my hand to sink the whole Island in the ocean."[13]

Two months earlier, on June 21, 1775, Jefferson had taken his seat in Congress.[14] On May 11, Congress had received tidings of the commencement of hostilities at Lexington and Concord on April 19; and on June 5, George Washington had been chosen as general "to command all the continental forces, raised, or to be raised, for the defence of American liberty." On June 23, a committee was appointed to draw up a declaration on taking up arms, to be published by General Washington. On June 24, the committee reported; on June 26, their report was recommitted, Dickinson and Jefferson being added to the committee. On July 6, the declaration was again reported, and was agreed to. It was followed, two days later, by an address to the inhabitants of Great Britain. To gratify Dickinson, a further petition to the King had been adopted on July 5. In all these state papers, Congress explicitly and repeatedly declared that the Colonies desired to maintain their union with Great Britain, but to do so upon "terms of just and equal liberty."[15]

[12] *Ibid.*, 58, 102.

[13] Jefferson, *Works*, II, 136. From the summer of 1768 when troops were sent to America, Samuel Adams had been convinced of the necessity of independence. William V. Wells, *Life and Public Services of Samuel Adams*, I, 172, 207.

[14] *Journals*, II, 101.

[15] *Ibid.*, 171. See also *ibid.*, 155, 160–61, 170, and Jefferson, *Papers*, I, 187–219.

Yet, while the Congress was thus indulging Dickinson and other conservatives in their insistence upon exhausting every possible mode of recourse in order to obtain redress and reconciliation through the traditional procedures of the English constitution, independence was rapidly becoming inevitable. Those who were in arms against the King's troops could not long continue to profess loyalty to the crown. New England and Virginia were in the forefront as separation from Great Britain approached. Pennsylvania and the middle colonies hung back, fearing revolutionary changes in their own internal government if the ties with England were severed.

When Congress reconvened on September 5, 1775, no answer had been received to Dickinson's petition. Though couched, Americans believed, "in the most humble terms," it was spurned by the British monarch, who, on the very day he was to have received it, issued instead his proclamation of August 23, 1775, declaring that "open and avowed rebellion" existed in the Colonies. On October 26, 1775, in a warlike speech from the throne upon the opening of Parliament, he denounced "those who have long too successfully laboured to inflame my people in America, by gross misrepresentations, and to infuse into their minds a system of opinions repugnant to the true constitution of the Colonies, and to their subordinate relation to Great Britain." They now "openly avow their revolt, hostility, and rebellion." The King charged the colonists with aiming at independence: "The rebellious war now levied is become more general, and is manifestly carried on for the purpose of establishing an independent Empire." Hence it had become "the part of wisdom . . . to put a speedy end to these disorders by the most decisive exertions." He announced measures for strengthening the land and naval forces, as well as receipt of "the most friendly offers of foreign assistance; and if I shall make any treaties in consequence thereof, they shall be laid before you."[16]

In 1776 public sentiment in favor of independence grew rapidly. The King's speech was received in Congress on January 8, 1776, at the same time as news that the British had burned Norfolk. Two days later Tom Paine's *Common Sense* was pub-

[16] Peter Force, *American Archives* (4th series), III, 240–41; VI, 1–3.

lished in Philadelphia. This pamphlet inflamed the popular mind, and contributed substantially to hasten the advent of independence. In striking language Paine demonstrated that there was not a single advantage to be gained by connection with England. Further impetus toward separation was given by passage of an act of Parliament (16 Geo. III, c.5) declaring the Colonies out of the king's protection. This statute prohibited all trade with America and authorized forfeiture of captured ships and cargoes as enemy property. It was approved by the King on December 22, 1775, and on February 27, 1776, a copy of it which Robert Morris received from a correspondent in England was read in Congress.[17]

On May 15, 1776, two noteworthy events occurred.

The first of these was the adoption by Congress of a preamble (prepared by John Adams)[18] to its resolution of May 10, 1776, calling upon the states to "take up government" and suppress all exercise of authority under the crown. On May 16, 1775, Massachusetts had asked Congress for "your most explicit advice respecting the taking up and exercising the powers of civil government, wch. we think absolutely necessary for the Salvation of our country." Congress by resolution of June 9, 1775, replied that an assembly of representatives and a council should be chosen to "exercise the powers of Government, until a Governor of his Majesty's appointment, will consent to govern the colony according to its charter." Similar advice had also been given to New Hampshire, South Carolina, and Virginia, recommending the establishment of "such form of government as in their judgment will best produce the happiness of the people, and most effectually secure peace and good order in the colony, during the continuance of the present dispute between Great Britain and these colonies." The general resolution of May 10, 1776, was in-

[17] *Common Sense*, 37 ff.; "Diary of Richard Smith in the Continental Congress, 1775–1776," *American Historical Review*, Vol. I, No. 2 (April, 1896), 506. Regarding debates on independence, see *ibid.*, 495, 502, 505, 512, 514. John Adams belittled Paine's pamphlet as containing nothing that had not previously been uttered in Congress. *Works*, II, 412, 507, 509. But the effect on public opinion of a political utterance does not necessarily depend upon its novelty or its originality.

[18] *Journals*, IV, 357–58. See John Adams, *Works*, II, 489–91, 510.

tended to enable the advocates of independence in Pennsylvania to oust the conservative government there which derived its authority from the charter granted to William Penn by the king.[19]

The resolution, with its significant preamble, reads as follows:

> Whereas his Britannic Majesty, in conjunction with the lords and commons of Great Britain, has, by a late act of Parliament, excluded the inhabitants of these United Colonies from the protection of his crown; And whereas, no answer, whatever, to the humble petitions of the colonies for redress of grievances and reconciliation with Great Britain has been or is likely to be given; but, the whole force of that kingdom, aided by foreign mercenaries, is to be exerted for the destruction of the good people of these colonies; And whereas, it appears absolutely irreconcileable to reason and good Conscience, for the people of these colonies now to take the oaths and affirmations necessary for the support of any government under the crown of Great Britain, and it is necessary that the exercise of every kind of authority under the said crown should be totally suppressed, and all the powers of government exerted, under the authority of the people of the colonies, for the preservation of internal peace, virtue, and good order, as well as for the defence of their lives, liberties, and properties, against the hostile invasions and cruel depredations of their enemies; therefore,
>
> *Resolved,* That it be recommended to the respective assemblies and conventions of the United Colonies, where no government sufficient to the exigencies of their affairs have been hitherto established, to adopt such government as shall, in the opinion of the representatives of the people, best conduce to the happiness and safety of their constituents in particular, and America in general.[20]

Impressed with the decisive importance of this resolution, John Adams "thought it was independence itself." Referring to it, together with the resolutions of the Continental Congress in

[19] *Journals*, II, 77, 84; III, 319, 326–27, 403–404; John P. Selsam, *The Pennsylvania Constitution of 1776*, 112–16; Merrill Jensen, *The Articles of Confederation*, 96–98.

[20] *Journals*, IV, 342. For comments of Adams, see John H. Hazelton, *The Declaration of Independence: Its History*, 105–106, 448.

1774, of which also he acknowledged himself to be the author, he questioned "Whether the Declaration of Independence of 4 July 1776 is any thing more than a juvenile declamation founded on those two documents."

The other important event of May 15 was the adoption on that day by the convention in Williamsburg of resolutions instructing the Virginia delegates in Congress to "propose to that respectable body to declare the United Colonies free and independent states," and also to assent to measures "for forming foreign alliances, and a confederation of the colonies," provided that "the power of forming government for, and the regulations of the internal concerns of each colony, be left to the respective colonial legislatures."[21]

On June 7, 1776, pursuant to these instructions the senior delegate from Virginia, Richard Henry Lee, offered a threefold resolution upon the subject of independence, foreign alliances, and confederation.[22] The resolution was seconded by John Adams of Massachusetts. After two days of debate, consideration of it was postponed for several weeks in order that public opinion in the more conservative colonies might mature. Meanwhile, lest any time should be lost, a committee was appointed to draw up a declaration to accompany the resolution of independence in the event of its adoption. This committee, chosen on June 11, 1776, was composed of Thomas Jefferson, John Adams, Benjamin Franklin, Roger Sherman, and Robert R. Livingston.

The task of preparing a draft of the Declaration fell to Jefferson. He wrote this paper in the parlor on the second floor of the house where he had lodgings, located at the southwest corner of Seventh and Market Streets. He used a folding desk which had been designed by himself and made by a Philadelphia cabinetmaker. The house was demolished in 1883; the desk is now on display in the National Museum at Washington.

[21] *The Proceedings of the Convention of Delegates, Held at the Capitol, in the City of Williamsburg, in the Colony of Virginia, on Monday the 6th of May, 1776,* 32. On March 5, 1776, John Page had written to Jefferson, and Charles Lee had written to Richard Henry Lee, urging an immediate declaration of independence. Hazelton, *The Declaration of Independence,* 72.

[22] Julian P. Boyd, *The Declaration of Independence* (2nd ed.), Document III; *Journals,* V, 425-26.

After submitting his draft to Adams and Franklin, who contributed a number of amendments, Jefferson reported it to the committee. The committee's report to Congress was made on June 28, 1776, and was laid on the table until after the Lee resolution was adopted on July 2, 1776. The Declaration was then debated, and was adopted on July 4.[23]

During the debate in committee of the whole on Lee's resolution for independence, nine states voted in the affirmative, but South Carolina and Pennsylvania voted against it. Delaware's two members present were divided, and New York abstained. At the request of the South Carolina delegates, the final vote by the Congress was put off until the following day, July 2. On that day, South Carolina joined the majority, in the interest of unanimity. Delaware's vote was likewise cast in the affirmative as the result of Caesar Rodney's arrival in response to Thomas McKean's urgent summons. Pennsylvania, too, was counted in favor of independence; for John Dickinson and Robert Morris absented themselves, and the two other opponents of independence in the delegation (Thomas Willing and Charles Humphreys) were outnumbered by the minority of three supporters of the resolution (Benjamin Franklin, James Wilson, and John Morton). New York did not participate in the decision. The delegates of that state, though personally favoring independence and convinced that their constituents did also, had received no official instructions authorizing them to vote for the Declaration.[24]

On June 8, 1776, the Pennsylvania assembly had removed the restrictions imposed in its prior instructions of November 9, 1775, which prohibited assent to any propositions "that may cause or lead to a separation from our Mother Country" or to a change in the state government under William Penn's charter. In Pennsylvania there were complications because the alignment of parties was such that to support independence meant also to favor replacing the time-honored charter by an untried and demo-

[23] *Journals*, V, 428-29, 431, 491, 510; Dumbauld, *Thomas Jefferson, American Tourist*, 50; Thomas Jefferson, *Writings*, XVIII, 349-50; Jefferson, *Works*, XII, 307, 413-14.

[24] Hazelton, *The Declaration of Independence*, 63, 163-66, 198, 300, 303. For convenience, I sometimes refer to colonies as "states" even before their independence.

cratic form of state government. Since independence could not be declared without Pennsylvania, the friends of independence in Congress joined with the radical faction in that state and overthrew the charter government. But so much partisan dissension was created that Pennsylvania's effectiveness during the Revolutionary War was paralyzed.[25] This was part of the price paid by American patriots to establish the nation's freedom.

Texts of the Declaration

THERE are three official texts of the Declaration of Independence. Of these, the earliest, and apparently the most authoritative,[26] is the broadside, printed by John Dunlap at Philadelphia on the night of July 4, 1776, and wafered into the so-called "rough" Journal of the Congress at its appropriate place among the proceedings of that date. A second official text is found in the so-called "corrected" Journal, written out in the hand of Charles Thomson, the secretary of Congress. Both the rough and the corrected Journals are preserved among the Continental Congress papers in the Library of Congress at Washington. The third official text is the copy engrossed on parchment, and bearing the familiar autographs of the signers.[27] It is this copy which is most frequently reproduced, and which is enshrined for public display

[25] *Ibid.*, 17, 188–90; Charles J. Stillé, "Pennsylvania and the Declaration of Independence," *Pennsylvania Magazine of History and Biography*, Vol. XIII, No. 4 (January, 1890), 422, 425; Stillé, *The Life and Times of John Dickinson*, 170, 173, 175, 178–81, 187; Charles H. Lincoln, *The Revolutionary Movement in Pennsylvania*, 14, 189, 207, 226, 250, 277 282, 285–87; Selsam, *The Pennsylvania Constitution of 1776*, 92, 97, 112–21, 132, 183, 253; Jensen, *The Articles of Confederation*, 14–15, 20, 93, 98, 101, 110, 239, 244.

[26] Three words omitted in the corrected Journal (see pages 124, 139, and 149, below) seem to be errors in copying rather than corrections. One of these omissions has hitherto escaped notice. Cf. Carl Becker, *The Declaration of Independence*, 173; Boyd, *The Declaration of Independence* (2nd ed.), 17. Boyd states that the rough Journal is followed in the Revised Statutes of 1878, though the Supreme Court has on occasion relied on the engrossed copy. There is no uniformity among the texts in capitalization, punctuation, and similar points of style.

[27] All three texts are printed in Hazelton, *The Declaration of Independence*, 306–43.

in the Library of Congress at Washington in company with the Constitution of the United States.

The Dunlap broadside was printed by order of Congress and under the supervision of the committee which drew up and reported the Declaration to Congress. On July 4, 1776, it was

> Ordered That the declaration be authenticated & printed
>
> That the committee appointed to prepare the declaration superintend & correct the press.[28]

The committee's report, with the amendments made by Congress, would be the most authentic official text; but no such document, if it ever existed, is now known to be extant; quite possibly it was used as printer's copy and was not preserved. The printed broadside thus seems to me to be the truest embodiment we can now find of the Declaration as adopted by Congress, and I have therefore chosen it as the text to be used in this volume.

It is possible that the Dunlap broadside was printed from the Rough Draft itself. John Adams, at the age of eighty-eight, wrote to Timothy Pickering on August 6, 1822: "We were all in haste; Congress was impatient and the Instrument was reported, I believe in Jefferson's hand writing as he first drew it." But Jefferson's recollection differed from that of Adams, and he states that he made "a fair copy, reported it to the Committee, and from them, unaltered to Congress."[29] It seems unlikely that Jefferson would have made fair copies to send to Wythe and Lee,[30] while reporting to Congress the Rough Draft. Moreover, it seems probable that the autograph signatures of John Hancock and Charles Thomson would appear on the copy authenticated by them for printing.

On July 19, 1776, Congress resolved:

> That the Declaration passed on the 4th be fairly engrossed on parchment with the title and stile of "The unanimous declaration of the thirteen united states of America" & that the same when engrossed be signed by every member of Congress.

---

[28] *Journals*, V, 516; Hazelton, *The Declaration of Independence*, 170.
[29] Hazelton, *The Declaration of Independence*, 143–44.
[30] See page 20 below.

This resolution directing that the title be changed to show that the instrument was the unanimous declaration of all thirteen states was adopted four days after the assent of New York to the Declaration had been made known to Congress. On August 2, 1776, "The declaration of Independence being engrossed & compared at the table was signed by the Members."[31]

Perhaps at that time Jefferson added the two corrections on the parchment copy, which appear to be in his handwriting. The letters "en" are inserted in the clause "He has dissolved Repres[en]tative Houses repeatedly," and the word "only" in "Our repeated Petitions have been answered [only] by repeated injury."

Some signatures were added after that date. Many of the signers were not in Congress on July 4, 1776, when the Declaration was adopted. Some members who had voted for the adoption of the Declaration were not signers. Possibly signature was regarded as a test of loyalty to the revolutionary cause, and as exposing signers to the danger of punishment for treason in the event of English victory in the war. It may also have been regarded as necessary (like signatures to a treaty) in order to render the Declaration binding upon the individual states.

As Jefferson aptly remarked, "the sentiments of men are known not only by what they receive, but what they reject also."[32] It is therefore of interest to note the extent of the revision to which the Declaration was subjected during the course of its evolution.

Congress, as well as members of the committee, made numerous modifications in the text as prepared by Jefferson. There were eighty-six changes made, eliminating 480 words, and leaving 1,337 words in the Declaration.[33] These amendments strengthened the literary effect of the document,[34] though Jefferson did

[31] *Journals*, V, 590–91, 626; Hazelton, *The Declaration of Independence*, 204, 208, 532–34.

[32] *Works*, I, 33–34.

[33] Boyd, *The Declaration of Independence*, (2nd ed.), 42.

[34] John Quincy Adams, *Memoirs*, VIII, 281–83. Regarding the literary qualities of the Declaration, see Moses C. Tyler, *The Literary History of the American Revolution*, I, 494–521; Becker, *The Declaration of Independence*, 194–223.

THOMAS JEFFERSON
from Charles Willson Peale's portrait

not relish them, particularly the omission of those passages condemning the slave trade. "The pusillanimous idea that we had friends in England worth keeping terms with still haunted the minds of many. For this reason those passages which conveyed censures on the people of England were struck out, lest they should give offence," Jefferson explained. "When the Declaration of Independence was under the consideration of Congress, there were two or three unlucky expressions in it which gave offence to some members. The words 'Scotch and other foreign auxiliaries' excited the ire of a gentleman or two of that country. Severe strictures on the conduct of the British king, in negativing our repeated repeals of the law which permitted the importation of slaves, were disapproved by some Southern gentlemen whose reflections were not yet matured to the full abhorrence of that traffic. Altho' the offensive expressions were immediately yielded, these gentlemen continued their depredations on other parts of the instrument."[35]

During this debate, Jefferson was sitting by Benjamin Franklin, who consoled him by telling the story of John Thompson, the hatter. That tradesman, having composed an inscription for the signboard of his shop, submitted it to his friends for criticism; after their amendments nothing remained but his name and the picture of a hat.

From manuscripts that have been preserved, the several stages through which the Declaration passed before attaining its final form may be traced. The most fascinating of these significant documents is Jefferson's so-called "Rough Draft,"[36] on which he noted all the changes made by himself and his colleagues on the committee, as well as those made by the Congress.[37] Two other copies of the Declaration furnish important evidence throwing

[35] *Works*, I, 33; XII, 109–10.

[36] The Rough Draft, preserved among the Jefferson papers in the Library of Congress, is reproduced in Boyd, *The Declaration of Independence* (2nd ed.), Document V. It was a "fair copy" of an earlier draft or notes for a draft. Julian P. Boyd, "New Light on Jefferson and His Great Task," *The New York Times Magazine*, April 13, 1947, 17 ff.

[37] Even after the final text had been adopted by Congress, Jefferson seems to have made one change which appears in the Rough Draft and nowhere else: "our repeated petitions have been answered only by repeated injuries." All other texts read "injury."

light upon the evolution of the text. One is in the handwriting of John Adams, and was taken at an early stage of the drafting.[38] By comparison of this copy with the Rough Draft, it is possible to reconstruct the version first submitted by Jefferson to Franklin and Adams.[39] The other is in Jefferson's handwriting, and was sent by him on July 8, 1776, to Richard Henry Lee.[40] It indicates the changes made by Congress. By comparison of this and other similar copies[41] with the Rough Draft and with the official texts, the wording of the Declaration as reported to Congress by the committee on June 28, 1776, can be ascertained.

Jefferson's own first version of the Declaration was not the fruit of mere ratiocination, although he asserts that he "turned to neither book nor pamphlet while writing it."[42] It followed familiar precedents. It invoked the hallowed heritage of English constitutional history. It voiced the doctrines of accepted political philosophers, particularly John Locke, whose writings were esteemed as authoritative expressions of established principles. It recapitulated the substance of previous state papers, some of them drafted by Jefferson himself, in which the American contentions had been formulated during the course of the prolonged dispute with England.

[38] The Adams copy, preserved in the Adams family papers, is reproduced in Boyd, *The Declaration of Independence* (2nd ed.), Document IV. It is printed in Jefferson, *Works*, II, 199–217; *Journals*, V, 491–502; Hazelton, *The Declaration of Independence*, 306–43.

[39] Boyd, *The Declaration of Independence* (2nd ed.), 19–21, and Becker, *The Declaration of Independence*, 141–51, print versions of the Declaration as prepared by Jefferson before submitting it to Adams and Franklin. See also Jefferson, *Works*, II, 199–217, and Jefferson, *Papers*, I, 423–27.

[40] Jefferson, *Works*, II, 217. In 1825 the Lee copy was presented to the American Philosophical Society in Philadelphia, by R. H. Lee's grandson. It is printed in Hazelton, *The Declaration of Independence*, 306–43, and is reproduced in Boyd, *The Declaration of Independence* (2nd ed.), Document VI.

[41] Jefferson's *Autobiography* contains the text of the Declaration in his handwriting, showing the changes made by Congress. *Works*, I, 35–42. A copy of it, made for Madison and enclosed in a letter dated June 1, 1783, is in the Madison papers in the Library of Congress. Boyd, *The Declaration of Independence* (2nd ed.), Document VIII. A copy similar to the Lee draft was also sent by Jefferson early in July, 1776, to George Wythe. This is now in the New York Public Library. *Ibid.*, Document VII. Another (incomplete) draft in Jefferson's handwriting sent by him to Edmund Pendleton, is in the Massachusetts Historical Society. *Ibid.*, Document IX.

[42] *Works*, XII, 307.

Jefferson was unquestionably familiar with the Stamp Act resolutions, the Massachusetts circular letter of February 11, 1768, to the assemblies of the other colonies, the resolutions, petitions, and addresses of the Continental Congress, the declaration on taking up arms, the replies to Lord North's conciliatory motion,[43] and similar utterances which would inevitably leave their trace upon a document intended to be an authentic "expression of the American mind."[44] Particularly significant, it seems to me, are two sources upon which Jefferson manifestly drew when drafting the Declaration: his *Summary View of the Rights of British America*, published in 1774, and his preamble to the Virginia constitution of 1776.[45] In each of these is contained a recital of grievances which closely parallels the Declaration of Independence.

The catalogue of charges against George III in Jefferson's preamble to the Virginia constitution strongly indicates, by its rhythm and phrasing, that it was patterned upon passages in the English bill of rights[46] where the people of England were enumerating the reasons which justified their choice of new rulers in place of James II. The misdeeds of that monarch were there itemized in a fashion strikingly similar to Jefferson's impressive indictment of George III.

To the men of 1776 the "glorious revolution" of 1688 in England was a vivid and thrilling reality. It had occurred less than a century before; it was a living and vital force in their daily

[43] Jefferson drew an address of June 12, 1775, to Governor Dunmore, replying on behalf of Virginia to Lord North's proposal, and prepared a similar draft for the Continental Congress. *Works*, II, 101–106, 125–33.

[44] *Ibid.*, XII, 409.

[45] *Ibid.*, II, 158–65; Boyd, *The Declaration of Independence* (2nd ed.), Document II. The preamble from Jefferson's proposed constitution was received by the Virginia Convention in time to be combined with the declaration of rights and frame of government prepared by George Mason. Hence persons unfamiliar with these circumstances have sometimes charged Jefferson with copying the Declaration of Independence from Mason. Its paragraph on the foundations of government parallels the Virginia bill of rights. William F. Dana, "The Declaration of Independence," *Harvard Law Review*, Vol. XIII, No. 5 (January, 1900), 327–28.

[46] 1 Wm. and Mary, 2 sess., c. 2. The conduct of James II was discussed during debate in Congress on the question of independence. Jefferson, *Works*, I, 25. Cf. the charges and sentence pronounced against Charles I. Rushworth, *Historical Collections*, VII, 1396–98, 1418–19. See Jefferson, *Papers*, I, 329–86.

conduct and thinking; for them it had not become what it is to us today, a dimly remembered story of ancient events in the history of a foreign nation, buried in obscure chronicles of the past, and familiar only to historians.[47] Americans resisting what they regarded as infringements of their constitutional rights conscientiously studied the precedents and principles enshrined in English history. They felt themselves to be following in the path of Coke, Pym, Hampden, Eliot, Milton, Algernon Sidney, and the patriots who decapitated Charles I in 1649 and deposed James II in 1689 for violations of the compact between king and people.

A well-known writer on English law observes that "the controversy between Great Britain and her colonies, like the controversy between Parliament and the Stuart kings, was cast into a legal mold. The events of, and the arguments used in, the earlier, were always present to the minds of the parties of the later, controversy." Thus Jefferson records that when preparing an earlier state paper in Virginia, he used "Rushworth, whom we rummaged over for the revolutionary precedents & forms of the Puritans of that day."[48] Likewise the conservative John Dickinson was particularly insistent upon pursuing meticulously the procedure established by English precedents for vindicating the rights of the people. New England and Virginia statesmen were more willing to make arguments relying upon the natural rights of mankind, in addition to those based upon the British constitution and Colonial charters.[49]

Jefferson's use of the bill of rights as pattern for his preamble makes it evident that in his judgment George III could rightfully be "deposed from the kingly office" by Americans because the situation was identical, constitutionally, with that which had existed when James II was lawfully ousted by English patriots. The

---

[47] For the course of English constitutional struggles, and the overthrow of the theory of divine right of kings, see the works by Allen, Gooch, Dunning, and Mullett, listed in the Bibliography.

[48] William S. Holdsworth, *A History of English Law*, XII, 116; Jefferson, *Works*, I, 12. Rushworth's *Historical Collections*, "Setting forth only Matter of Fact in Order of Time, Without *Observation* or *Reflection*," cover the period from 1618 to the execution of Charles I.

[49] Dickinson, *Letters from a Farmer*, 34; Stillé, *The Life and Times of John Dickinson*, 29, 84, 129, 134.

same inference may be drawn from those passages in the Declaration of Independence which show the influence of Locke, for that philosopher's political treatises were written as a defense of the revolutionists who placed William and Mary on the throne "abandoned" by James II.

Besides inspiring the American votaries of liberty in 1776, the English bill of rights proclaimed in 1689 was the pattern and prototype for the constitutional safeguards added a century later to the Constitution of the United States at the insistence of Jefferson and other friends of democratic government.[50]

[50] The lack of a bill of rights was one of the principal defects which Jefferson found in the Constitution as prepared by the convention at Philadelphia in 1787. *Works*, V, 371–72, 426–28, 461–64. The first ten amendments to the Constitution were added in 1789.

THE DECLARATION
OF INDEPENDENCE

In CONGRESS, JULY 4, 1776.
A DECLARATION
By the REPRESENTATIVES of the
UNITED STATES OF AMERICA,
In GENERAL CONGRESS assembled.

The corrected Journal reads:

A Declaration by the representatives of the united states of America in Congress assembled.

The parchment copy reads:

IN CONGRESS, JULY 4, 1776.

The unanimous Declaration of the thirteen united States of America,

Omission of the word "general" in the corrected Journal may reflect a suggestion made in Congress that this word be struck out. But the amendment, if accepted by Congress, failed to be incorporated in the Dunlap broadside. Nor was it noted by Jefferson on the Rough Draft, or on the Lee copy or the Pendleton copy. The change is indicated, however, on the Wythe copy, the copy in Jefferson's *Autobiography*, and the copy made for Madison.

The United States of America

The first time that the name "United States of America" is known to have been officially used was in the Declaration of Independence. Before that the expression "United Colonies" was generally employed.[1]

[1] Edmund C. Burnett, "The Name 'United States of America,'" *American Historical Review*, Vol. XXXI, No. 1 (October, 1925), 79.

Another interesting fact is that the name "Declaration of Independence" nowhere appears in the document itself, although three varying forms of title are given in the three official texts.

It is possible that Jefferson started to write "A Declaration of Independence," because the Rough Draft shows that "of" was first written, after the word "Declaration," instead of "by."

Did Jefferson make this alteration in wording "because he thought, perhaps, that the basic philosophy of government and of rights in this document was more inclusive than a mere declaration of the severance of dependency on Great Britain"?[2] This attractive hypothesis could well be true, because it was Jefferson's democratic philosophy, proclaimed in striking fashion in the Declaration as well as in other utterances, which had the effect of ensuring that the American Revolution resulted in the establishment of republican government throughout the United States, rather than in the mere multiplication of monarchies.

One often forgets that in Jefferson's day most persons of voting age had been born as subjects of a kingdom, and were accustomed to the ceremonies and trappings of royalty. That form of government was then widely prevalent in the world; indeed, the framers of the Constitution of the United States in 1787 had to recur frequently in the course of their debates to Greek and Roman antiquity for examples of republican institutions. It was far from being inevitable that separation from England should mean the realization of democracy in America. That independence and popular government became inseparable objectives in American political life was due in large part to their effective combination in the unforgettable Declaration penned by Jefferson.[3]

In changing "title & stile" of the Declaration when ordering it engrossed on parchment, Congress emphasized the unanimity among the thirteen states on whose behalf it was proclaimed to the world. This change was ordered on July 19, 1776, four days after the assent of New York was made known to the Congress.

[2] Boyd, *The Declaration of Independence* (2nd ed.), 22.

[3] See speech of Abraham Lincoln at Independence Hall on February 22, 1861. Cf. Dana, "The Declaration of Independence," *Harvard Law Review*, Vol. XIII, No. 5 (January, 1900), 331, 336–37, 340–41.

Although the delegates of that state had not been authorized to vote for the Declaration when it was adopted on July 4, it was approved a week afterward by the New York convention meeting at White Plains, whose resolutions on the subject were read in Congress on July 15. Thus did the thirteen states unanimously "join in the general voice of America."

The Preamble

W*HEN in the Course of human Events, it becomes neces-sary for one People to dissolve the Political Bands which have connected them with another, and to assume among the Powers of the Earth, the separate and equal Station to which the Laws of Nature and of Nature's God entitle them, a decent Respect to the Opinions of Mankind requires that they should declare the causes which impel them to the Separation.*

The Rough Draft reads "for a people to advance from that sub-ordination in which they have hitherto remained, & to assume among the powers of the earth the equal & independent station to which the laws of nature & of nature's God entitle them, a decent respect for the opinions of mankind requires that they should declare the causes which impel them to the change." The revisions in this paragraph were made by the committee.

one People

Whether the American Colonies (collectively or individual-ly) constituted "one people," and Great Britain "another," or whether the British Empire as a whole was a single people, is of course one of the controversial issues which led to the American Revolution.

Thomas Hutchinson, former royal governor of Massachu-setts, who had constantly been embroiled with the assembly dur-ing his term of office, said in a pamphlet attacking the Americans: "They begin . . . with a false hypothesis, That the Colonies are one *distinct people*, and the kingdom another, connected by politi-cal bands." Hutchinson considered it impertinent to discuss un-der what circumstances a *whole people* is justified in rising up against a government.[1]

From the English point of view the Colonies were a part of the empire; Parliament possessed law-making powers over the entire empire; therefore the colonists were a turbulent and re-

[1] *Strictures upon the Declaration of the Congress at Philadelphia*, 9 (here-after referred to as *Strictures*).

bellious set of disaffected subjects when they objected to taxation and other acts of legislation by the home government. To the Americans, on the other hand, their own legislative assemblies occupied the position which the English Parliament had come to hold in the esteem of the people as the protector of their historically recognized liberties against the unconstitutional usurpations of a tyrannous monarch and his subservient officials.[2]

The struggle which thus began as a controversy over the proper interpretation of the constitutional law of the British Empire, a dispute concerning the appropriate allocation of governmental powers within the polity, soon became a civil war.[3] Neither side, however, grasped the full possibilities of federalism as a desirable solution of their political difficulties, even though in actual practice, as distinguished from English theory, a considerable measure of federalism, roughly parallel to later American constitutional developments, had already grown up within the British Empire.[4] American political thinkers had long contended that constitutionally the Colonies were connected with the central government only through the crown, and that their own local assemblies were exclusively vested with certain powers, particularly that of taxation.[5]

Implicit in the Declaration is the "social compact" theory, that a people is a political organization of persons, who, having theretofore lived in a "state of nature" without being united by any political bonds, associate themselves together and bind themselves by compact for the purpose of establishing government. It

[2] The English and American views were expressed in a multitude of political pamphlets, a number of which are listed in the Bibliography.

[3] After the Declaration of Independence it became an international war. American courts regarded the United States as sovereign and independent after July 4, 1776; English courts dated recognition of that status from the peace treaty of September 3, 1783. *Ware* v. *Hylton*, 3 Dall. 199, 225 (1796); *Inglis* v. *Sailor's Snug Harbor*, 3 Pet. 99, 121 (1830).

[4] The essence of federalism is political decentralization, based upon recognition of the principle that governmental powers may be limited in extent, and may be distributed among various holders. Andrew C. McLaughlin, *A Constitutional History of the United States*, 25, 125; Randolph G. Adams, *Political Ideas of the American Revolution*, 185.

[5] Edward S. Corwin, "The 'Higher Law' Background of American Constitutional Law," *Harvard Law Review*, Vol. XLII, No. 2 (December, 1928), 402.

is the voluntary union of individuals that creates the "people" or state for secular political purposes, just as under the Puritan covenant theory it creates the church for religious purposes.[6]

Did the Declaration create one people or thirteen? One, says a prominent German theorist.[7] But this view seems contrary to historically established political facts.[8] The record of events indicates that each state was a separate people; they participated in a scheme of joint action in order to manage more effectively their common concerns, especially the conduct of belligerent operations.[9] The only legal connection uniting the thirteen colonies before the Revolution was with the crown, not with each other. Dickinson and other conservatives desired the establishment of a federation before a Declaration of Independence.[10]

When Dickinson says that the Colonies were "as much dependent on Great Britain as one free people could be on another," he assumes that America is one people, that England is another, and that each is free.[11] Similarly when Jefferson in the *Summary View* says of the act of Parliament suspending the New York Assembly that "One free and independent legislature hereby takes upon itself to suspend the powers of another, free and independent

[6] Andrew C. McLaughlin, *The Foundations of American Constitutionalism*, 12, 20.

[7] Hermann E. von Holst, *The Constitutional and Political History of the United States*, I, 5–6. His theory is that the independence of each state resulted solely from the action of Congress; and that the powers of Congress were unlimited, because it was an illegal or revolutionary body. But this assumption is fallacious. Because the powers of Congress were new and not derived from the authority of the royal government's law, it does not follow that they were necessarily unlimited.

[8] For example, Virginia declared its own independence before the Continental Congress acted.

[9] James Brown Scott, *Sovereign States and Suits before Arbitral Tribunals and Courts of Justice*, 37–40, 56; Claude H. Van Tyne, "Sovereignty in the American Revolution," *American Historical Review*, Vol. XII, No. 3 (April, 1907), 533–35, 537; John Quincy Adams, *Parties in the United States*, 3–4; Jensen, *The Articles of Confederation*, 162, 176; *Ware* v. *Hylton*, 3 Dall. 199, 224, 232 (1796); Griffith J. McRee, *Life and Correspondence of James Iredell*, I, 311; Jefferson, *A Summary View of the Rights of British America*, 7 (hereafter cited as *Summary View*).

[10] Hazelton, *The Declaration of Independence*, 108, 112, 397; Stillé, *The Life and Times of John Dickinson*, 371; Jensen, *The Articles of Confederation*, 91.

[11] Becker, *The Declaration of Independence*, 96–97.

as itself,"[12] he is asserting that New York and Great Britain are separate peoples, each free and independent.

While secretary of state, Jefferson stressed, during the course of negotiations with Spain, that "The several states, now composing the U. S. of America, were, from their first establishment, separate & distinct societies, dependant [*sic*] on no other society of men whatever. They continued at the head of their respective governments the executive magistrate who presided over the one they had left, & thereby secured in effect a constant amity with that nation. . . . The part which our chief magistrate took in a war waged against us by the nation among whom he resided, obliged us to discontinue him, & to name one within every state."

On another occasion, Jefferson remarked that "before the revolution, the nation of Virginia had, by the organs they then thought proper to constitute, established a system of laws . . . When, by the declaration of Independence, they chose to abolish their former organs of declaring their will, . . . the nation was not dissolved, was not annihilated . . . . The common law, therefore, which was not in force when we landed here, nor till we had formed ourselves into a nation, and had manifested by the organs we constituted that the common law was to be our law, continued to be our law, because the nation continued in being, & because though it changed the organs for the future declarations of its will, yet it did not change its former declarations that the common law was it's law. . . . Before the revolution there existed no such nation as the US; they then first associated as a nation, but for special purposes only. They had all their laws to make, as Virginia had on her first establishment as a nation."[13]

The use of the words "one People" does not warrant the conclusion that the Declaration envisaged a single, sovereign state in America. It is not said that the entire population of the Colonies constituted "one People." Each colony individually could be considered as a "People" dissolving the "Political Bands" connecting it with England. Here, as elsewhere in the Declaration, the term "People"[14] seems to be used as a collective noun to designate

[12] Page 12.
[13] *Works*, VI, 415–16; IX, 75–76. See also pages 67–68, 73, 78–79 below.
[14] The word "People" occurs ten times in the Declaration: besides the ref-

an aggregation of individuals; a plural pronoun is used in the same sentence with reference to the singular antecedent "one People." The text speaks of the political bands connecting "them" with another people, and of the station to which the laws of nature entitle "them," and states that "they" should declare the causes which impel "them" to separation. Likewise in the concluding paragraph of the Declaration, where the Colonies are proclaimed by authority of "the good People" thereof to be free and independent states, the plural pronoun again appears (though now it refers to a plural antecedent): "they" are absolved from allegiance to the British crown; political connection between "them" and Great Britain is dissolved; "they" have full power to do what independent states may of right do. From this paragraph it would seem that each colony is regarded as a separate state, free and independent in its own right.

separate and equal Station

Upon their complete separation from the British state, the American Colonies immediately became "subjects of international law." In that capacity they were entitled to the sovereignty and equality which the law of nations attributes to each member of the international community. As stated by Justice James Wilson, "When the United States declared their independence, they were bound to receive the law of nations, in its modern state of purity and refinement."[1] In the language of a modern English jurist, "They became bound by international law just in the same way as an individual is bound by municipal law—that is to say, as an inevitable result of birth into a society ruled by that law."[2]

The equality of states is one of the basic doctrines of international law. The principle was succinctly and forcefully ex-

---

erence to "one People" in the opening paragraph, we find "the Right of the People" to alter government; "large Districts of People, unless those People"; "Invasions on the Rights of the People"; legislative powers "returned to the People at large"; officers "to harrass our People"; "the Lives of our People"; "the Ruler of a free People"; "by authority of the good People of these Colonies."

[1] *Ware* v. *Hylton,* 3 Dall. 199, 281 (1796).

[2] Sir John Fischer Williams, *Chapters on Current International Law and the League of Nations,* 14.

Folding desk, on which the Declaration of Independence
was written

pressed in Chief Justice John Marshall's statement that "Russia and Geneva have equal rights."[3]

The doctrine arose when the "state of nature" and "law of nature" concepts were applied to nations and not merely to individuals. It was first formulated by Pufendorf and was popularized by Vattel.[4] Jefferson was familiar with the works of these writers, and cited them frequently. As the first secretary of state of the United States, in George Washington's administration, he himself contributed greatly to the development of modern international law.[5]

The problems arising from the theoretical legal equality of states and their actual inequality in population, wealth, power, and other important respects, which confronted the Colonies during the Revolution and Constitutional Convention in 1787, are similar to those which today confront nations seeking to establish just and effective international government. Hence American experience affords a valuable precedent for statesmen dealing with questions of international organization.[6]

the Laws of Nature

By this expression Jefferson here seems to refer to the law of nations, or international law, as it is more commonly called today.

International law regulates the relations between independent sovereign nations and is distinguished from the internal or "municipal" law which is in force within a single nation. As has been

---

[3] *The Antelope*, 10 Wheat. 66, 122 (1825). See also Samuel Pufendorf, *De Jure Naturae et Gentium*, II, 226, 330, 342 (Book II, c. iii, § 23; Book III, c.ii, §§ 1, 8); and Emmerich de Vattel, *The Law of Nations*, III, 7 (Introduction, § 18). Vattel taught that nations "are by nature equal."

[4] Edwin D. Dickinson, *The Equality of States in International Law*, 82, 97–98.

[5] Charles M. Wiltse, "Thomas Jefferson on the Law of Nations," *American Journal of International Law*, Vol. XXIX, No. 1 (January, 1935), 66–81; Charles G. Fenwick, "The Authority of Vattel," *American Political Science Review*, Vol. VII, No. 3 (August, 1913), 395–410; Charles M. Thomas, *American Neutrality in 1793*. Jefferson's copy of the first edition of Vattel is in the Library of Congress.

[6] Charles Warren, *The Supreme Court and Sovereign States*; Carl Van Doren, *The Great Rehearsal*.

seen above, the equality of states is one of the basic doctrines of international law, and Jefferson is here invoking on behalf of the American Colonies the status accorded by international law to sovereign states. After independence was attained, the relations between the American Colonies and Great Britain would no longer be a matter of internal constitutional law within the British Empire, but would be governed by international law.

The terms "law of nature" and "natural law" are not ordinarily limited to international law, but embody a theory of political society which relates to the philosophical foundations of law and government within an individual state as well as between states.

While the expression "international law" seems to have been originated by Jeremy Bentham,[1] and the body of law to which it refers did not come into existence until the establishment of the modern state-system which after the Reformation replaced the earlier unity of Christendom under the Papacy and Holy Roman Empire,[2] the "law of nature" concept upon which the structure of international law was originally erected is of much more venerable antiquity.

In large measure, international law originated as an application of natural-law concepts to the sphere of international relations. International law was brought into being when the jurist-theologians of the sixteenth and seventeenth centuries who deduced principles of natural law from reason or divine will proceeded to formulate rules which were binding on the sovereign in his relations with other sovereigns as well as those applicable to his relations with his own subjects and to their relations with each other. This method of treating together international law, constitutional law, and political theory was long fashionable (for example, it appears in the law lectures given by James Wilson in the winter of 1790–91 at what is now the University of Pennsylvania while he was a justice of the Supreme Court of the United States). The "law of nature" philosophy held its ground longer in the field of international law than elsewhere, when

[1] Jeremy Bentham, *An Introduction to the Principles of Morals and Legislation*, 326 (chap. XVII, § 25, written in 1780, first published in 1789).

[2] James L. Brierly, *The Law of Nations*, 9.

36

"positivist" views began to supplant it. Rationalistic and ethical speculation was more necessary there as a creative force, because international law was a less matured legal system containing fewer well-developed rules of positive law. Nations are still largely in a "state of nature" with respect to each other, with little government or law established to curb their selfish conduct.[3]

The origin of natural-law theories may be traced back to Aristotle, Cicero, philosophers and jurists of the Roman empire, mediaeval writers such as Thomas Aquinas, and other predecessors of the English revolutionists who inspired Jefferson.[4]

The belief that certain legally binding rules of human conduct can be derived by reason from the nature of man and the universe in which he lives constitutes the essence of the natural-rights philosophy, a philosophy which has never wholly lost its appeal. To holders of this view, the commands of "positive law," composed of specific enactments created as the product of a historical process, are binding only when not in conflict with the fundamental dictates of "natural law."

The fact that the legal validity of a rule is thus made to depend upon its moral justice is the source both of the strength and of the weakness of the natural-law philosophy. That there are laws of higher authority than those that emanate from the established governmental mechanisms of politically organized society has always been a heartening belief, of inestimable value in arousing and inspiring through the ages the courageous struggles of those who have defended righteousness and resisted tyranny, from the times of Antigone and Brutus to the times of Jefferson and of the European underground in World War II.

But the weakness of the natural-law philosophy is that, in the

[3] Edward Dumbauld, "The Place of Philosophy in International Law," *University of Pennsylvania Law Review*, Vol. LXXXIII, No. 5 (March, 1935), 594–95; *The Works of the Honourable James Wilson*, I, 45, 145, 150; Roscoe Pound, "The End of Law as Developed in Juristic Thought," *Harvard Law Review*, Vol. XXVII, No. 1 (May, 1914), 615–16; E. D. Dickinson, *The Equality of States*, 33, 37, 44.

[4] James Sullivan, "The Antecedents of the Declaration of Independence," *Annual Report of the American Historical Association for 1902*, I, 66–85; E. D. Dickinson, *The Equality of States*, 6–29; Sir Frederick Pollock, "The History of the Law of Nature," *Columbia Law Review*, Vol. I, No. 1 (January, 1901), 11–32; Vol. II, No. 3 (March, 1902), 131–43.

opinion of modern "positivist" jurists, it confounds the separate realms of law and morals,[5] ignores the plain distinction between "is" and "ought to be," and is technically untenable because it makes legality depend upon nonlegal criteria. Another shortcoming of natural law is that its successful operation is impossible if there is a wide divergence of view as to what is or is not just. Most persons are apt to treat as an immutable law of nature whatever they happen to be accustomed to.[6]

To the positivist, law is created as the product of an established law-making process (such as enactment by Parliament, decision by courts, or command issued by an emperor or military ruler); whatever is produced in due conformity with that process is law, regardless of its wisdom or foolishness as a matter of policy, its soundness or unsoundness as a matter of logic, its justice or injustice as a matter of ethics. The content of law is something to be ascertained by determining whether or not as a matter of historical fact the proper procedure has been pursued and the requisite formalities completed in order to give the force of law to a particular rule of conduct. Good laws and bad laws are equally law. A nation may prohibit or permit intoxicating liquors as it pleases; it may admit or exclude immigrants as it sees fit; it may adopt free trade or a protective tariff as it chooses; it may require, permit, or forbid racial segregation in accordance with its own standards of propriety. What was lawful in Germany in 1938, for example, the positivist believes, is to be learned by scrutiny of the law which as a matter of historical fact was in force at that time and place, by examination of the output of the law-making agencies of Hitler's Germany. It is not to be ascertained by determining what the officials of a victorious army of occupation ten years later believe would have been just and humane conduct a decade

[5] See Roscoe Pound, *Law and Morals*. So strict is the distinction drawn between law and morals by the analytical school of jurisprudence (of which the English writer John Austin was the founder) that it treats international law as a form of morality rather than as law. The modern Vienna school of Hans Kelsen likewise distinguishes sharply between law (a normative system) and other social disciplines, but concedes that international law can be part of the legal system.

[6] Oliver W. Holmes, Jr., *Collected Legal Papers*, 312; Roscoe Pound, "Liberty of Contract," *Yale Law Journal*, Vol. XVIII, No. 7 (May, 1909), 466.

before. Such beliefs, however, may constitute the law of Germany in 1948, in the positivist's estimation, if they are in fact applied as the rule by which war criminals are then and there punished.

Similarly, to a positivist, it would be folly to assert, at the constitutional level, that the people are entitled to participate in the process of law-making. Whether the constitution of a particular state does or does not, as a matter of positive law, provide for popular participation in the legislative function is simply a matter to be ascertained by analysis of the existing constitution; whatever rules are duly enacted by the organs entrusted with law-making power are deemed laws by the positivist, and the absence of consent by the governed does not deprive of validity a law so enacted any more than does the circumstance that the law may be unjust, unwise, or immoral. Indeed, to say that law is binding only when made by consent of the people is perhaps merely a special case of the proposition that no law is binding if it is contrary to natural justice.

The positivist would emphasize that the first Continental Congress claimed the right of the people to participate in making their laws merely as being "the foundation of *English* liberty and of all *free* government" [italics supplied]. But not all government is free government, and it is only by historical accident, the positivist would say, that the English monarchs happened to need more money than they could conveniently extract from the upper classes and therefore in exchange for grants from the commons gave to the representatives of the people a recognized place in the composition of Parliament and an important share in the legislative power under the English constitution.

The Declaration of Independence, therefore, was transcending the provisions of positive law when it claimed as natural rights of all mankind, in reliance upon "the laws of nature and of nature's God," the traditionally recognized privileges such as legislation based upon the consent of the governed which were historically the special heritage of *English* liberty and philosophically the peculiar characteristic of *free* government. Believers in the Declaration's philosophy maintained that certain rights were inherent in the people. This was the converse of the monarchists' position, criticized by the eminent English jurist John Selden, that certain prerogatives were inherent in the crown: "A king that claims privileges in his own country because they have them in another is just as a cook that claims fees in one lord's house because they are allowed in another. If the master of the house will yield them, well and good. . . . To know what obedience is due to the prince, you must look into the contract betwixt him and the people; as if you would know what rent is due from the tenant to the landlord, you must look into the lease."[7]

Positivism would assert that people have the right to legislate for themselves only where the particular constitution under which they live actually accords them that right. Positivism has the advantage of being able to contemplate with equanimity and analyze with impartiality legal systems which are, or are not, free governments. And history shows that the majority of mankind, whether viewed with respect to time or place, have lived under governments that cannot be characterized as free.

Jefferson said that history was nothing but a record of bad government.[8] The few centuries during which English and American governments have given a measure of freedom to their people may be regarded as exceptional. It is perhaps possible that free government will prove incompatible with survival in an atomic age.[9] In any event, it seems plain that no people will long enjoy liberty who do not cherish it and vigilantly battle for it. In Jefferson's apt phrase, "we are not to expect to be translated from despotism to liberty in a feather-bed."[10]

To some extent every system of positive law admits an element of "natural law" where it gives discretionary power to judges or officials to make decisions, not in conformity with a fixed and pre-established rule, but in accordance with equity, reasonableness, "natural justice," "due process of law," "general

[7] *The Table Talk of John Selden*, 90, 191.

[8] *Works*, X, 416.

[9] See Edward S. Corwin, *Total War and the Constitution*, 130, 180.

[10] *Works*, VI, 40.

[11] Regarding the incorporation of natural-law concepts into certain doctrines of American constitutional law (particularly "liberty," "property," and "due process of law" as interpreted in Supreme Court decisions), see Charles G. Haines, *The Revival of Natural Law Concepts*, 40-41, 212-13, 347. Concern-

principles of law," or other similarly vague criteria.[11] Thus the Interstate Commerce Commission is empowered to prescribe "reasonable" railroad rates; courts may determine what is a reasonable time, or reasonable value; juries in negligence cases apply the standard of "due care," i.e., what a "reasonable and prudent man" would have done under the circumstances. Such subsidiary or "interstitial" adoption of natural law as part of positive law is quite different from reliance upon natural law as a justification for violation of express positive law.

When James Otis declared that an act of Parliament contrary to natural law is void, he was uttering nonsense, to the positivist way of thinking, if it be assumed that the positive law rule of the English constitution then was what it has now plainly become in England.[12] On the other hand, a similar assertion made in the last quarter of the nineteenth century regarding an act of Congress might have been regarded as a statement of the positive law in force in the United States.[13] For United States courts as a matter of actual fact were exercising the power to declare unconstitutional an act of Congress or of a state legislature which they regarded as contrary to natural justice and hence as violating the "due process" clause of the Constitution. But suppose that at that time and place some venturesome nineteenth-century Otis had had the hardihood to declare that a Supreme Court decision contrary to natural justice was void? Such a statement would have

ing the power of international courts to apply "general principles of law," see Edward Dumbauld, *Interim Measures of Protection in International Controversies*, 177.

[12] Regarding the omnipotence of Parliament, see Albert V. Dicey, *Introduction to the Study of the Law of the Constitution.* Cf. Jefferson, *Writings*, XVI, 42. Far from an act of Parliament against Magna Carta being regarded as void, Parliament repealed part of Magna Carta itself in 1887. Max Radin, "The Myth of Magna Carta," *Harvard Law Review*, Vol. LX, No. 7 (September, 1947), 1090–91.

[13] See *Loan Association* v. *Topeka*, 20 Wall. 655 (1874) and authorities cited in Haines, *The Revival of Natural Law Concepts*, regarding the adoption of natural law in "due process" cases. See also Benjamin F. Wright, Jr., *American Interpretations of Natural Law.* As illustrative of natural-law notions in current constitutional decisions of the Supreme Court, see *Adamson* v. *California*, 332 U. S. 46, 53–54, 65, 70, 75 (1947); *Bute* v. *Illinois*, 333 U. S. 640, 659 (1948).

[14] John Chipman Gray, *The Nature and Sources of the Law* (2nd ed.), 102, 125.

had no meaning for a positivist, like John Chipman Gray.[14] For how could a decision be void which was obviously valid positive law because the Supreme Court had just pronounced it?

The law of nature philosophy proclaimed by Jefferson in the Declaration of Independence was unmistakably based upon the teachings of John Locke,[15] Algernon Sidney, and other defenders of English liberty as established by the "glorious revolution" of 1688. But Jefferson was doubtless aware also of the ancient lineage of that philosophy. He himself included Aristotle and Cicero among the "elementary books of public right" from which it might have been derived.

Aristotelian teaching spoke of "natural" justice as distinguished from "conventional" justice. This distinction is similar to that in Anglo-American law between *malum prohibitum* and *malum in se,* or between offenses which are mere technical violations of arbitrary statutory enactment and those which evince moral turpitude. A familiar passage reads:

> Political justice is partly natural and partly conventional. The part which is natural is that which has the same authority everywhere. . . .
>
> It is the opinion of some people that all the rules of justice are conventional, because that which is natural is immutable and has the same authority everywhere, as fire burns equally here and in Persia, but they see the rules of justice continually altering.
>
> . . . Nevertheless there is a justice which is, as well as a justice which is not, natural.[16]

The Stoic philosophers developed the idea of an ethical and rational law of nature, applicable everywhere and always. In Cicero this ideal of a cosmopolitan natural law, based upon reason and common to all peoples, was eloquently expressed:

[15] "Richard Henry Lee charged it as copied from Locke's treatise on government." Jefferson, *Works*, XII, 307. On a subsequent occasion, Jefferson said: "All its authority rests then on the harmonizing sentiments of the day, whether expressed in conversation, in letters, printed essays, or in the elementary books of public right, as Aristotle, Cicero, Locke, Sidney, &c." *Ibid.*, 409.

[16] *The Nicomachean Ethics of Aristotle,* 159–60. See Sir Frederick Pollock, *Essays in the Law,* 33.

True law is, indeed, right reason, conformable to nature, pervading all things, constant, eternal. . . . It is not lawful to alter this law, to derogate from it, or to repeal it. Nor can we possibly be absolved from this law, either by the senate or the people; . . . nor will it be one law for Rome and another for Athens; one thing today and another tomorrow; but it is a law eternal and unchangeable for all people and in every age . . . .[17]

In Rome the concept of natural law was transmitted from the philosophers to the jurists, who tended to identify this universal law based upon reason and nature (*jus naturale*) with a branch of Roman positive law known as the "law of nations" (*jus gentium*). This was made up of the rules applicable to lawsuits involving foreigners. The Roman "civil law" (*jus civile, jus Quiritium*) applied only to Roman citizens. The *praetor peregrinus*, an official having jurisdiction of cases concerning foreigners, did not apply that law. Instead, he had recourse to the *jus gentium*, a body of law considered suitable for application regardless of the citizenship of the litigants, because it embodied such generally recognized principles of natural justice and equity as could properly be regarded as universal and common to all mankind.

The distinction between *jus naturale* and *jus gentium* lay in the fact that the former was an ideal, ethical system based upon reason and justice, while the latter embodied rules established by general custom or usage. Thus it was recognized by Roman jurists that slavery was an institution which existed under the *jus gentium* because it was generally practiced, whereas by the *jus naturale* all men are born free and equal.[18]

When modern international law arose, and the law of nature was applied by analogy to the relationships between states, the

[17] *The Republic of Cicero*, 256–57:

Est quidem vera lex recta ratio, naturae congruens, diffusa in omnes, constans, sempiterna. . . Huic legi nec obrogari fas est, neque derogari ex hac aliquid licet, neque tota abrogari potest: nec vero aut per senatum aut per populum solvi hac lege possumus: neque est quaerendus explanator aut interpres ejus alius: nec erit alia lex Romae, alia Athenis; alia nunc, alia posthac; sed et omnes gentes et omni tempore una lex et sempiterna et immutabilis continebit.

[18] Passages to this effect in Justinian's codification of Roman law include Inst. 1, 2, 2; Inst. 1, 3, 2; Inst. 1, 5, pr.; Dig. 1, 1, 4; Dig. 1, 5, 4, 1; Dig. 1, 6, 1, 1; Dig. 12, 6, 64; Dig. 50, 17, 32.

conclusion was logically reached, which Vattel proclaimed, to the effect that "nations are free, independent, and equal."[19]

Jefferson could therefore invoke "the Laws of Nature and of Nature's God" as entitling the independent American Colonies to a "separate and equal Station" among "the Powers of the Earth" composing the family of nations governed by international law.

Nature's God

In view of Jefferson's familiarity with the writings of Lord Bolingbroke and the poet Alexander Pope,[1] it is quite possible that this expression was borrowed from those writers. In Pope's *Essay on Man* occur the lines:

> *Slave to no sect, who takes no private road,*
> *But looks through Nature up to Nature's God.*[2]

And Bolingbroke expresses the same sentiment:

It is the modest, not the presumptuous, inquirer who makes a real and safe progress in the discovery of divine truths. One follows Nature and Nature's God; that is, he follows God in his works and in his word.[3]

Bolingbroke in a passage which Jefferson copied as a youth in his literary commonplace book declared: "I say that the law of Nature is the law of God."[4] Pope likewise in the *Essay on Man* (in a strain akin to Locke rather than Hobbes) proclaimed that:

> *The state of Nature was the reign of God.*[5]

So, too, the learned and witty English jurist Selden said: "I cannot fancy to myself what the law of nature means, but the law of God."[6]

[19] Vattel, *The Law of Nations*, III, 7 (Introduction, §§ 18, 21).
[1] Gilbert Chinard, *The Literary Bible of Thomas Jefferson*, 20–21, 40, 130.
[2] Page 47 (Epistle IV, lines 331–32).
[3] *The Works of Lord Bolingbroke*, III, 62.
[4] *Ibid.*, IV, 239. See also *ibid.*, 159, 275.
[5] Page 31 (Epistle III, line 148).
[6] *Table Talk*, 101. See Pollock, *Essays in the Law*, 40–43.

44

It seems evident that Jefferson in similar fashion here identifies natural law and divine law. He treats them both as a single concept; he has no occasion to concern himself with the distinctions between them which Thomas Aquinas, Grotius, and other theological writers had elaborated.[7]

the Opinions of Mankind

With this passage of the Declaration should be compared Woodrow Wilson's fine statement of the international objectives of American foreign policy:

> What we seek is the reign of law, based upon the consent of the governed, and sustained by the organized opinion of mankind.[1]

The importance of public opinion as the basis of all government, even the most absolute despotism, was recognized by the Scottish philosopher David Hume, with whose writings Jefferson was familiar:

> Nothing is more surprising to those, who consider human Affairs with a Philosophical Eye, than to see the Easiness with which the many are governed by the few; and to observe the implicite Submission with which Men resign their own Sentiments and Passions to those of their Rulers. When we enquire by what Means this Wonder is brought about, we shall find, that as FORCE is always on the Side of the Governed, the Governors have nothing to support them but OPINION. 'Tis therefore on Opinion only that Government is founded; and this Maxim extends to the most despotic and most military governments, as well as to the most free and most popular. The *Soldan* of Ægypt, or the *Emperor* of *Rome*, might drive his harmless Subjects, like brute Beasts, against their Sentiments and Inclination: But he must, at least, have led his *Mamalukes*, or *Praetorian Bands*, like Men, by their Opinion.[2]

[7] Hugo Grotius *De Jure Belli ac Pacis*, II, 38, 44 (Book I, c. ix, xiii); *Basic Writings of Saint Thomas Aquinas*, II, 748 (*Summa Theologica, prima secundae, quaestio xci*).

[1] Address at Mount Vernon, July 4, 1918.

[2] *Essays, Moral and Political*, 39. Adrienne Koch, *The Philosophy of Thomas Jefferson*, 15, 194. See also Montesquieu, *Lettres Persanes*, I, 163 (letter lxxxiii); and Sir James Fitzjames Stephen, *Horae Sabbaticae*, III, 349.

Jefferson's faith in the power of public opinion strongly appears in a statement made during his presidency that England "is now a living example that no nation however powerful, any more than an individual, can be unjust with impunity. Sooner or later, public opinion, an instrument merely moral in the beginning, will find occasion physically to inflict it's sentences on the unjust."[3]

In commenting while secretary of state upon the consequences of nonfulfillment of treaty obligations, he observed: "But the tribunal of our consciences remains, & that also of the opinion of the world."[4]

"Opinion is power," Jefferson said on another occasion.[5] Political institutions could be remoulded so as to abolish war, poverty, disease, or any other evil due to human conduct, "if the people wished."[6]

Separation

This euphemism denotes an act of revolution, resulting in the creation of a new state (or states) out of territory formerly part of another sovereignty. It differs from a mere overthrow of the existing government without changing the boundaries of the state (for example, England's "glorious revolution" of 1688). It is also distinguishable from the opposite process of "consolidation," where a new state is formed by the merger of two or more existing states (for example, the unification of Italy in the nineteenth century, or the replacement of the Articles of Confederation by the Constitution of the United States, if the view is taken that before but not after the adoption of the Constitution each state was a sovereign "subject of international law").

[3] *Works*, X, 77. Cf. Justice Robert H. Jackson's address of April 13, 1945, in *Proceedings of the Washington Meeting of the American Society of International Law* (1945), 17.

[4] *Works*, VII, 286.

[5] *Writings*, XIV, 396.

[6] Archibald MacLeish, *A Time to Speak*, 3. According to MacLeish, it is a poet's function to stir the imagination of the people. In this sense Jefferson was a poet when he spoke the sentiment of America. "Indeed, the Declaration of Independence is a kind of war-song; it is a stately and passionate chant of human freedom; it is a prose lyric of civil and military heroism." Tyler, *The Literary History of the American Revolution*, I, 521.

"Separation" is synonymous with "secession." The latter term attained wide use in connection with events leading up to the war of 1861–65. According to a prominent nineteenth-century German political theorist, Jefferson was "the father of the doctrine of nullification," the precursor of secession.[1] Earlier in the century, however, when South Carolina nullificationists such as Calhoun and Hayne sought to buttress their doctrines by claiming the authority of Jefferson in their support, James Madison stoutly resisted their attempts to "father" such a theory upon Jefferson.[2]

The Kentucky and Virginia Resolutions of 1798, declaring the Alien and Sedition Laws (1 Stat. 577, 596) unconstitutional, were regarded by nullificationists as a precedent for their claim that a single state, being sovereign, could nullify acts of the federal government. Madison pointed out that the Virginia Resolutions, of which he himself had been the draftsman, gave no support to such a contention; and that even in Jefferson's draft of the Kentucky Resolutions, where the word "nullification" appears, it is plain that the expression refers not to a constitutional right of resistance to federal authority, such as the nullificationists claimed, but to a "natural right" to resist unconstitutional oppression or tyranny.[3] Such a natural right, Madison asserted, was enjoyed not only by an individual state, but by any portion thereof so aggrieved, even a single county or citizen.[4]

It was of such an *ultima ratio* or "appeal to Heaven," in Locke's phrase,[5] that Jefferson was thinking when he wrote in his draft of the Kentucky Resolutions that "this commonwealth is determined, as it doubts not its co-States are, to submit to un-

---

[1] Holst, *The Constitutional and Political History of the United States*, I, 149.

[2] "And this newfangled theory is attempted to be fathered on Mr. Jefferson the apostle of republicanism, and whose own words declare that 'acquiescence in the decision of the majority is the vital principle of it.'" Madison, *Writings*, IX, 589. See also Andrew C. McLaughlin, "American History and American Democracy," *American Historical Review*, Vol. XX, No. 2 (January, 1915), 266.

[3] *Writings*, IX, 589. Madison emphasized that the Virginia Resolutions were intentionally so worded as to speak of the "states" (in the plural number), not of a single state. *Ibid.*, 387–89, 444, 483, 490, 496.

[4] *Ibid.*, 348, 353. See also *ibid.*, 387, 398, 471, 483.

[5] John Locke, *Two Treatises of Government*, (edited by William S. Carpenter, 1924), 203, 241. (All citations are to this edition.)

47

delegated, and consequently unlimited powers in no man, or body of men on earth: that . . . where powers are assumed which have not been delegated, a nullification of the act is the rightful remedy: that every State has a natural right in cases not within the compact (*casus non foederis*) to nullify of their own authority all assumptions of power by others within their limits; that without this right they would be under the dominion, absolute and unlimited, of whosoever might exercise this right of judgment for them: that nevertheless, this commonwealth from motives of regard and respect for its co-States, has wished to communicate with them . . . they alone being parties to the compact, . . . Congress being not a party, but merely the creature of the compact."[6]

Jefferson himself viewed with horror the thought of disunity or secession. He declared that "to render us again one people, acting as one nation, should be the object of every man really a patriot. I am satisfied it can be done, and I own that the day which should convince me of the contrary would be the bitterest of my life."[7]

"Separation," whether from the American Union or from the British Empire, was justifiable, in Jefferson's eyes, only when necessary to avert a calamity yet greater, that of "submission to a government of unlimited powers."[8] Here, as throughout his life, Jefferson remained faithful to the principles of the American Revolution. With these utterances of his, compare the assertion made by the Massachusetts House on January 26, 1773, declaring that "nothing is more evident than that any people, who are subject to the unlimited power of another, must be in a state of abject slavery."[9]

Similarly, under Madison's conception of the social-compact philosophy, secession was legitimate only if the seceding party were relieved of the obligations of the contract either by reason of violations committed by other parties, or by the consent of the other parties.[10] This view may be compared with Locke's statements to the effect that while government exists, its legislative

[6] *Works,* VIII, 471–72.
[7] *Works,* IX, 283. See also *ibid.,* VIII, 432; XII, 420, 425–26.
[8] *Ibid.,* XII, 420; Adrienne Koch, *Jefferson and Madison,* 197, 219.
[9] *Massachusetts State Papers* (edited by Alden Bradford), 353.
[10] Madison, *Writings,* IX, 355–56, 495, 513.

power is supreme, and the "power of the people" can never be directly operative until the government is dissolved; but that in the event of a breach of trust by the government, its power is forfeited to the people, who then resume their original liberty and may frame a new government as they see fit.[11]

"Natural law" rules resembling those governing the many topics treated in the law of contracts[12] must thus be presupposed in order to make the social-compact theory workable. If past consent did not create a continuing obligation, or if the consent of a majority did not create an obligation upon the minority, government would be a practical impossibility.

The compact theory has been put forward as the basis both of municipal and of international obligation. Many writers have sought to rest the binding force of international law as a whole upon the consent of states, treating custom as "tacit consent." Others regard the rule *pacta sunt servanda* as the fundamental or "constitutional" rule (*Grundnorm*) of international law, from which other international obligations derive their validity.[13]

But as Hume wisely inquires, why should promises be binding? Would it not be simpler to base the validity of laws directly upon their social necessity rather than upon an intermediate rule that gives binding force to whatever has received assent? "If the Reason is askt of that Obedience, which we are bound to pay to Government, I readily answer; *because Society cou'd not otherwise subsist*: And this Answer is clear and intelligible to all Mankind. Your Answer is *because we show'd keep our Word.... You find yourself embarrass'd when 'tis asked you, why we are bound*

---

[11] *Two Treatises of Government*, 192–93, 228–29. This notion of Locke's may be derived from analogy to English real-property law, where an owner in fee simple may grant an estate of freehold and retain a reversionary interest, which will take effect in possession only at the expiration of the freehold estate or its forfeiture.

[12] For example, the formation, interpretation, performance, breach, rescission, and dissolution of contracts. Regarding the Anglo-American law of contracts, see the monumental treatise of Samuel Williston, *The Law of Contracts*. Similar rules of international law have been developed with regard to treaties. Brierly, *The Law of Nations*, 165; Samuel B. Crandall, *Treaties, Their Making and Enforcement*.

[13] Brierly, *The Law of Nations*, 37–39; Dumbauld, "The Place of Philosophy in International Law," *University of Pennsylvania Law Review*, Vol. LXXXIII, No. 5 (March, 1935), 597–601.

49

to keep our Word? And you can give no other Answer, but what would, immediately, without any Circuity, have accounted for our Obligation to Allegiance."[14]

Yet to one who believes that "the consent of the governed" is the only just basis of political authority, it seems plain that forcible prohibition of secession is the equivalent of conquest. And, as Jefferson said, "If there be one principle more deeply rooted than any other in the mind of every American, it is that we should have nothing to do with conquest."[15]

If "the earth belongs to the living and not to the dead," a people should not be compelled against their will to submit to an unacceptable government merely because their ancestors regarded it as desirable and consented to it.[16] The true legal analogy should be that of agency, rather than that of contract or trust; no misconduct or violation of plighted faith should be required as a condition precedent to a change in government. However virtuous and public-spirited the rulers of a state may be, the people should be free to cast them off and form a new regime whenever they see fit.

But even though it be conceded that a "people" may at any time "dissolve the political bands" which have theretofore confined them and may effect a "separation" from their former companions in the body politic, the troublesome question remains of determining what constitutes a "people."

To a large extent, the answer must be subjective and empirical. Any group whose sentiments of "belonging together" and *esprit de corps* are sufficiently strong to cause them to collaborate effectively in the establishment and maintenance of a sovereign and separate politically organized society is undoubtedly a "people." The fact of success in asserting and maintaining independence is the best proof of a people's nationhood and right to be independent.

The problem arose to plague the proponents of "self-determi-

[14] *Essays, Moral and Political*, 305.

[15] *Works*, VI, 293.

[16] A kindred idea is expressed in the remark of Justice Holmes: "It is revolting to have no better reason for a rule of law than that so it was laid down in the time of Henry IV." Holmes also observed that "continuity with the past is only a necessity and not a duty." *Collected Legal Papers*, 187, 211.

nation" of peoples at the peace conference in Paris following World War I. A similar question with respect to determining the appropriate unit for collective bargaining perplexes the administration of present-day labor laws. If the individualistic social-contract theory is accepted, it would seem that any single citizen desiring to separate from the state should be free to do so.[17] Jefferson regarded expatriation as a natural right of every individual, and a Virginia statute on the subject proclaimed the same view.[18]

In his *Summary View,* Jefferson wrote: "our ancestors, before their emigration to America, were the free inhabitants of the British dominions in Europe and possessed a right, which nature has given to all men, of departing from the country in which chance, not choice, has placed them, of going in quest of new habitations, and of there establishing new societies, under such laws and regulations as to them shall seem most likely to promote public happiness."[19]

[17] Madison distinguished secession from expatriation. *Writings,* IX, 497. See also *ibid.,* 353, 355–56.

[18] Jefferson, *Works,* I, 14; II, 64; IX, 341; X, 273; XII, 66; *The Statutes at Large,* Commonwealth of Virginia (edited by William W. Hening), X, 129 (act of 1779, c. lv).

[19] Page 6.

The American Philosophy of Government

WE hold these Truths to be self-evident, that all Men are created equal, that they are endowed by their Creator with certain unalienable Rights, that among these are Life, Liberty, and the Pursuit of Happiness—That to secure these Rights, Governments are instituted among Men, deriving their just Powers from the Consent of the Governed, that whenever any Form of Government becomes destructive of these Ends, it is the Right of the People to alter or to abolish it, and to institute new Government, laying its Foundation on such Principles, and organizing its Powers in such Form, as to them shall seem most likely to effect their Safety and Happiness. Prudence, indeed, will dictate that Governments long established should not be changed for light and transient Causes; and accordingly all Experience hath shewn, that Mankind are more disposed to suffer, while Evils are sufferable, than to right themselves by abolishing the Forms to which they are accustomed. But when a long Train of Abuses and Usurpations, pursuing invariably the same Object, evinces a Design to reduce them under absolute Despotism, it is their Right, it is their Duty, to throw off such Government, and to provide new Guards for their future Security. Such has been the patient Sufferance of these Colonies; and such is now the Necessity which constrains them to alter their former Systems of Government. The History of the present King of Great-Britain is a History of repeated Injuries and Usurpations, all having in direct Object the Establishment of an absolute Tyranny over these States. To prove this, let Facts be submitted to a candid World.

In the Rough Draft this paragraph reads:

"We hold these truths to be sacred & undeniable; that all men are created equal & independent, that from that equal creation they derive rights inherent & inalienable, among which are the preservation of life & liberty, & the pursuit of happiness; that to secure these ends, governments are instituted among men, deriving their just powers from the consent of the governed; that whenever any form of government shall become destructive of these ends, it is the right of the people to alter or to abolish it, & to institute new government, laying it's foundation on such principles & organising it's powers in such form, as to them shall seem most likely to effect their safety & happiness. Prudence indeed will dictate that governments long established should not be changed for light & transient causes: and accordingly all experience hath shewn that mankind are more disposed to suffer while evils are sufferable, than to right themselves by abolishing the forms to which they are accustomed. But when a long train of abuses & usurpations, begun at a distinguished period, & pursuing invariably the same object, evinces a design to subject them to arbitrary power, it is their right, it is their duty, to throw off such government & to provide new guards for their future security. Such has been the patient sufferance of these colonies; & such is now the necessity which constrains them to expunge their former systems of government. The history of his present majesty is a history of unremitting injuries and usurpations, among which no one fact stands single or solitary to contradict the uniform tenor of the rest, all of which have in direct object the establishment of an absolute tyranny over these states. To prove this, let facts be submitted to a candid world, for the truth of which we pledge a faith yet unsullied by falsehood."

The substitution of "self-evident" for "sacred & undeniable" was made by Jefferson or Franklin.

The committee, among other verbal improvements, changed "all men are created equal & independent" to "all Men are created equal"; and "from that equal creation they derive rights inherent & inalienable" to "they are endowed by their creator with equal rights, some of which are inherent & inalienable." This was further altered to read "they are endowed by their creator with inherent & inalienable rights." The committee also changed "the preservation of life & liberty, & the pursuit of happiness" to "Life, Liberty, & the Pursuit of Happiness"; and "secure these ends" to "secure these Rights." In the handwriting of Franklin, "power" is changed to "Despotism"; and in that of Adams, "his present majesty" is changed to "the present King of Great Britain."

The Congress changed "inherent & inalienable" to "certain unalienable" (although the printer, rather than Congress, may be responsible for the spelling "unalienable"); "expunge" to "alter"; and "unremitting" to "repeated." Congress also deleted "begun at a distinguished period," "among which appears no solitary fact to contradict the uniform tenor of the rest," and "for the truth of which we pledge a faith yet unsullied by falsehood."

these Truths

The principles set forth in this paragraph of the Declaration constitute the foundation of American political philosophy. It is because of what is here said that the Declaration has become immortal. To this it owes the strength of its perennial appeal to the hearts of American citizens.

These principles were not new. Wise men had for centuries recognized that the purpose of government, if it was to be ethically justifiable, was the welfare of the people governed.[1] The divine right of kings was an exploded doctrine, especially in England. Many writers had proclaimed that men were born free, and that their consent was an indispensable prerequisite to the establishment of political authority. Yet everywhere in Europe, royal and ecclesiastical oppression, the "government of wolves over sheep," inflicted misery upon a suffering populace, who looked with yearning to a land of hope and freedom across the seas.[2] "It is not enough, said Condorcet, that the rights of man 'should be written in the books of philosophers and in the hearts of virtuous

[1] Thus in Plato's *Republic* (I, 342, 345) it was stated that a ruler, insofar as he fulfills his true function as such, must seek to promote the welfare of the people governed, and not his own interest. *The Dialogues of Plato*, II, 164, 167.

[2] Dumbauld, *Thomas Jefferson, American Tourist*, 211–14.

men; it is necessary that ignorant or weak men should read them in the example of a great people. America has given us this example. The act which declares its independence is a simple and sublime exposition of those rights so sacred and so long forgotten.' "[3]

"These truths" have always been regarded by some scoffers not as truths but as falsehoods, or have been described as "glittering generalities." That expression was first used in a letter written by Rufus Choate in 1856. Choate, a Whig, supported Buchanan rather than Fillmore because he felt that the Republican party was sectional and that its victory would be harmful because to the South a Republican administration would appear as an alien and hostile government, "its constitution the glittering and sounding generalities of natural right which make up the Declaration of Independence."[4]

More recently, the Harvard philosopher Santayana has described the Declaration of Independence as "a piece of literature, a salad of illusions."[5]

Those who sought to justify slavery found it advisable to belittle the validity of the teachings of the Declaration, so contrary to their arguments in behalf of the "peculiar institution" they were defending.[6] They regarded the Declaration of Independence and the Virginia bill of rights, a kindred document, as inapplicable to slaves. George Wythe, Jefferson's law teacher, interpreted the latter declaration of rights as placing the burden of proof on the claimant whenever one person sought to hold another in slavery. In the Court of Appeals, Judge Tucker took a different view:

> I do not concur with the chancellor in his reasoning on the operation of the first clause of the Bill of Rights, which was notoriously framed with a cautious eye to this subject, and was meant to embrace the case of free citizens, or aliens only; and not by a side

[3] *Oeuvres*, VIII, 11, quoted in Becker, *The Declaration of Independence*, 230-31.

[4] Samuel G. Brown, *The Life of Rufus Choate*, 326.

[5] *The Middle Span*, 169.

[6] Tyler, *The Literary History of the American Revolution*, I, 503, 517; John Quincy Adams, *Memoirs*, IV, 492-93; VIII, 299-300.

wind to overturn the rights of property, and give freedom to those very people whom we have been compelled by imperious circumstances to retain, generally, in the same state of bondage that they were in at the revolution, in which they had no concern, agency, or interest.[7]

Other critics of the Declaration have charged that its "truths" were in fact platitudes and lacked originality. Richard Henry Lee complained that it was copied from Locke; John Adams observed that its sentiments had been hackneyed in Congress. Jefferson denied having consulted any books or pamphlets while writing it; he explained, however, that he did not consider it his duty to exclude every idea that had been previously uttered; in fact, he was giving voice to the generally held opinion of the American people. Indeed, on such an occasion, novelty is the last thing that would have been appropriate in a document of the sort which Jefferson was drafting. Both in style and in substance he was speaking the language of English law, of constitutional progress, of solemn precedent; he was the advocate of American rights at the bar of world public opinion.[8]

that all Men are created equal

This statement calls to mind the pronouncements of Roman jurists that under the law of nature all men are equal.[1] A similar sentiment from the Greek poet Euripides was copied by Jefferson as a youth into his literary commonplace book. A modern

[7] *Hudgins* v. *Wrights*, 1 Hening & Munford 134, 141 (Va., 1806). See also *Dred Scott* v. *Sandford*, 19 How. 393, 410 (1857); and Dana, "The Declaration of Independence," *Harvard Law Review*, Vol. XIII, No. 5 (January, 1900), 330.

[8] Jefferson, *Works*, XII, 307–308, 409; Tyler, *The Literary History of the American Revolution*, I, 504–505, 507, 519-21. Like Shakespeare's works, the Declaration now seems to be composed of familiar quotations. But it survives the test of being frequently read.

[1] Page 43 above. A memorable passage from the jurist Ulpian in Justinian's Digest reads: "*Quod attinet ad ius civile, servi pro nullis habentur: non tamen et iure naturali, quia, quod ad ius naturale attinet, omnes homines aequales sunt.*" Dig. 50, 17, 32. ("Insofar as pertains to civil law, slaves are considered as being nonentities; but it is not so by natural law, since, insofar as pertains to natural law, all men are equal.")

translator renders this passage "Nature gave men the law of equal rights."[2]

The same authorities held that under the law of nature all men are born free.[3] In 1770, before the General Court of Virginia, Jefferson had vainly though laboriously argued, citing Pufendorf, that statutes condemning to servitude the "child" of a mulatto would not operate to impose bondage upon a grandchild also, since "Under the law of nature, all men are born free."[4]

In like manner John Milton declared in *The Tenure of Kings and Magistrates,* an important pamphlet published in 1649 as a justification of the execution of Charles I: "No man who knows aught, can be so stupid to deny, that all men naturally were born free."[5]

The same principle is expressed in Locke:

> Men being, as has been said, by nature all free, equal, and independent, no one can be put out of this estate and subjected to the political power of another without his own consent. . . . When any number of men have so consented to make one community or government, they . . . make one body politic, wherein the majority have a right to act and conclude the rest.[6]

He repeats, a few pages later, that "men are naturally free" and that "the governments of the world, that were begun in peace, had

[2] Euripides, *Phoenissae,* line 538: "τὸ γὰρ ἴσον, νόμιμον ἀνθρώποις ἔφυ." Chinard, *The Literary Bible of Thomas Jefferson,* 97; *Euripides with an English Translation by Arthur S. Way,* 387.

[3] The origin of slavery was found in the law of nations, for by the law of nature all men were born free: "*iure enim naturali ab initio omnes homines liberi nascebantur.*" Inst. 1, 2, 2. See also Inst. 1, 3, 2; Dig. 1, 5, 4, 1; Dig. 12, 6, 64. Manumission was traced to the same origin by the jurist Ulpian: "*quae res a iure gentium originem sumpsit, utpote cum iure naturali omnes liberi nascerentur nec esset nota manumissio, cum servitus esset incognita.*" Dig. 1, 1, 4. See also Inst. 1, 5, pr.

[4] Argument in *Howell* v. *Netherland,* Jefferson, *Works,* I, 474, 480; Jefferson's *Reports,* 90, 92. Cf. George Mason's argument two years later in *Robin* v. *Hardaway,* Jefferson's *Reports,* 109, 122. See Pufendorf, *De Jure Naturae et Gentium,* II, 936, 942–43 (Book VI, c. iii, § § 4, 9), for the passage cited by Jefferson.

[5] *The Works of John Milton,* V, 8 (spelling modernized). Elsewhere Milton speaks of "men by nature free, born and created with a better title to their freedom than any king hath to his crown." *Ibid.,* 255 (spelling modernized).

[6] *Two Treatises of Government,* 164–65.

their beginning laid on that foundation, and were made by the consent of the people."[7]

Another eminent publicist with whose writings Jefferson was familiar, Vattel, also affirmed that "men are by nature equal."[8]

This passage of the Declaration inspired the noble sentiments expressed by Abraham Lincoln in his Gettysburg Address. On another noteworthy occasion, speaking at Independence Hall in Philadelphia on February 22, 1861, Lincoln acknowledged his indebtedness to the doctrines of Jefferson. He avowed that "all the political sentiments I entertain have been drawn . . . from the sentiments which originated and were given to the world from this hall. I have never had a feeling politically that did not spring from the sentiments embodied in the Declaration of Independence." Two years earlier, commemorating Jefferson's birthday, he wrote: "The principles of Jefferson are the definitions and axioms of free society. . . . All honor to Jefferson—to the man who, in the" midst of a struggle for national independence had the wisdom and foresight to enunciate "an abstract truth, applicable to all men and all times . . . so . . . that to-day and in all coming days it shall be a rebuke and a stumbling-block to the very harbingers of reappearing tyranny and oppression."

certain unalienable Rights

Such rights are regarded as "natural" rights not created by government,[1] but derived directly from "the Laws of Nature and of Nature's God." In his *Summary View*, Jefferson declared that "The God who gave us life gave us liberty at the same time; the

---

[7] *Ibid.*, 168. See also *ibid.*, 158. Regarding the historical origin of government, Hume remarked: "Almost all the Governments, which exist at present, or of which there remains any Record in Story, have been founded originally either on Usurpation, or Conquest, or both, without any Pretence of a fair Consent, or voluntary Subjection of the People." *Essays, Moral and Political,* 295.

[8] Vattel, *The Law of Nations,* III, 7 (Introduction, § 18). See page 35 above.

[1] The idea popularized in the Declaration that individuals possess rights not derived from the state is affecting modern international law relating to the status of persons without nationality. Philip C. Jessup, *A Modern Law of Nations,* 70, 90–91.

hand of force may destroy, but cannot disjoin them."[2] Commenting in his *Notes on Virginia* on the evil effects of slavery, he exclaimed: "And can the liberties of a nation be thought secure when we have removed their only firm basis, a conviction in the minds of the people that these liberties are of the gift of God? That they are not to be violated but with his wrath?"[3]

Speaking of expatriation, Jefferson later said: "The evidence of this natural right, like that of our right to life, liberty, the use of our faculties, the pursuit of happiness, is not left to the feeble and sophistical investigations of reason, but is impressed on the sense of every man. We do not claim these under the charters of kings or legislators, but under the King of kings."[4] In like manner Jefferson's political adversary Alexander Hamilton affirmed: "The rights of mankind are not to be rummaged for among old parchments or musty records. They are written, as with a sunbeam, in the whole volume of human nature, by the hand of Divinity itself, and can never be erased or obscured by mortal power."[5]

The rights specified in the Declaration are regarded as inalienable, because the people cannot deprive themselves of these inherent rights. Jefferson declared that "between society and society, or generation and generation there is no municipal obligation, no umpire but the law of nature. We seem not to have perceived that, by the law of nature, one generation is to another as one independent nation to another. . . . On similar ground it may be proved that no society can make a perpetual constitution, or even a perpetual law."

One generation cannot bind its successors; the earth belongs to the living and not to the dead.[6] "From the nature of things, every society must at all times possess within itself the sovereign power of legislation," Jefferson said. "Every man, and every body of men on earth, possesses the right of self-government. They receive it with their being from the hand of nature." Hence

[2] Page 23. This sentiment is voiced in the Latin motto *"Ab eo libertas a quo spiritus."*

[3] *Works*, IV, 83.

[4] *Ibid.*, XII, 66.

[5] Alexander Hamilton, *Works*, I, 113.

[6] Jefferson, *Works*, VI, 8, 10.

no citizen should be deprived, by restriction of suffrage to property owners, of his due "participation in the natural right of self-government."[7]

Life, Liberty, and the Pursuit of Happiness

The first Continental Congress in its resolutions of October 14, 1774, declared that the colonists were "entitled to life, liberty & property."[1] Less than two months previously, a Boston Committee of Correspondence had stated that "We are entitled to life liberty and the means of Sustenance." The Massachusetts Council on January 25, 1773, had asserted that "Life, liberty, property, and the disposal of that property, with our own consent, are natural rights."[2] The Fifth and Fourteenth Amendments to the Constitution of the United States prohibit deprivation of "life, liberty, or property" without due process of law.

In similar vein, Locke had spoken of preservation of their "lives, liberties, and fortunes" as the reason why men "quit the freedom of the state of Nature" and establish government. Locke declared that "government has no other end but the preservation of property." However, he defined property broadly, as including "life, liberty and estate." It comprises whatever a person has removed "out of the state that Nature hath provided and left it in" and "hath mixed his labour with."[3] Hence "the supreme power cannot take from any man any part of his property without his own consent. . . . For I have truly no property in that which another can by right take from me when he pleases against my consent."[4]

The phrase "pursuit of happiness" occurs in Locke's philosophical writings. It is also used by Dr. Samuel Johnson, and in other eighteenth-century works of literature.[5] Possibly Jefferson

[7] *Ibid.*, II, 83; VI, 98; XII, 353.

[1] *Journals*, I, 67.

[2] John C. Miller, *Origins of the American Revolution*, 370; *Massachusetts State Papers*, 350.

[3] *Two Treatises of Government*, 163–64, 159, 130.

[4] *Ibid.*, 187–88. The same sentiment recurs in John Dickinson, *Letters from a Farmer*, 137. See also *Massachusetts State Papers*, 126, 346.

[5] Herbert L. Ganter, "Jefferson's 'Pursuit of Happiness' and Some For-

used the phrase "pursuit of happiness" rather than "property" because he regarded property as a right derived from the state, whereas he was enumerating in the Declaration only "natural" rights, and "it is a moot question whether the origin of any kind of property is derived from nature at all."[6]

Justice Holmes ridiculed the idea of a right to life. Even before the general adoption of conscription,[7] he observed that soldiers were marched off to fight without regard to any supposed right to life. "The most fundamental of the supposed pre-existing rights—the right to life—is sacrificed without a scruple not only in war, but whenever the interest of society, that is, of the predominant power in the community, is thought to demand it."[8]

Similar objections may be made to the concept of "liberty." Law is inherently a restraint of liberty. Justice Holmes observed that "pretty much all law consists in forbidding men to do some things they want to do." A similar remark was made a century and a half previously by Thomas Hutchinson, native-born royal governor of Massachusetts: "Every restraint which men are laid under by a state or government, is a privation of part of their natural rights." And a Scottish critic of the Declaration wrote in August, 1776, that "every law, divine or human, that is or hath been in the world, is an abridgment of man's liberty."[9]

But if liberty is understood as being merely freedom to do whatever the law allows, it becomes meaningless. To be significant, "liberty" must have a "natural law" meaning ascertainable by reason. It must provide a criterion to which positive law should conform. However, the dogma of "liberty of contract" which

gotten Men," *The William and Mary Quarterly* (2nd series), Vol. XVI, No. 3 (July, 1936), 422–34; *ibid.*, No. 4 (October, 1936), 558–88. See also Norwood F. Allman, *Shanghai Lawyer*, 38.

[6] Jefferson, *Writings*, XIII, 333; Gilbert Chinard, *Thomas Jefferson, the Apostle of Americanism*, 84; *Mercoid Corp.* v. *Mid-Continent Co.*, 320 U. S. 661, 678 (1944); Koch, *Jefferson and Madison*, 64, 78, 82–88.

[7] Sustained by the Supreme Court in the *Selective Draft Cases*, 245 U. S. 366 (1918).

[8] Holmes, *Collected Legal Papers*, 304, 314; Holmes, *The Common Law*, 43; Edward Dumbauld, "Valedictory Opinions of Mr. Justice Holmes," *Michigan Law Review*, Vol. XLII, No. 6 (June, 1944), 1040.

[9] Holmes, dissenting in *Adkins* v. *Childrens' Hospital*, 261 U. S. 525, 568 (1923); *Massachusetts State Papers*, 340, 350; Hazelton, *The Declaration of Independence*, 479. See also Stephen, *Horae Sabbaticae*, II, 345–46.

certain past Supreme Court decisions adopted when construing the term "liberty" in the Constitution is now seen to be untenable.[10] The present court is adopting an equally unjustifiable interpretation of the Constitution by reading into the Fourteenth Amendment, to an undefined extent, the provisions of the bill of rights contained in the first ten amendments.[11]

The first ten amendments were directed solely against the federal government, as was correctly held in an opinion by Chief Justice John Marshall.[12] "Due process of law" in the Fourteenth Amendment, addressed to the states, should mean the same thing as the same words do in the Fifth Amendment, addressed to the federal government. The Fifth Amendment should not be construed as repetitious of the First. That the First Amendment did not bind the states is shown by the fact that in several New England states (as in Massachusetts until 1833) an established church was maintained long after adoption of the Constitution.[13]

Besides the protection which the Fifth and Fourteenth Amendments to the Constitution of the United States give to "life, liberty, and property," it should be noted that many states have expressly incorporated in their constitutions the substance of the Declaration's recognition of the citizen's right to "life, liberty, and the pursuit of happiness."[14] Moreover, the acts of Congress providing for the admission of some ten states to the Union contain provisions requiring that the state constitutions shall not be repugnant to the Declaration of Independence. Thus the act of April 19, 1864, for the admission of Nebraska provides "That the constitution, when formed, shall be republican, and

[10] Pound, "Liberty of Contract," *Yale Law Journal*, Vol. XVIII, No. 7 (May, 1909), 454–87.

[11] Charles Warren, "The New 'Liberty' under the Fourteenth Amendment," *Harvard Law Review*, Vol. XXXIX, No. 4 (February, 1926), 431–63; *Adamson* v. *California*, 332 U. S. 46, 53–54, 65, 70, 75 (1947); *Bute* v. *Illinois*, 333 U. S. 640, 659 (1948).

[12] *Barron* v. *Baltimore*, 7 Pet. 243, 247 (1833).

[13] Sanford H. Cobb, *The Rise of Religious Liberty in America*, 500–501, 515.

[14] Everett V. Abbott, "Inalienable Rights and the Eighteenth Amendment," *Columbia Law Review*, Vol. XX, No. 2 (February, 1920), 187, lists 31 states having such provisions in their constitutions.

not repugnant to the Constitution of the United States and the principles of the Declaration of Independence."[15]

to secure these Rights

The Declaration of Independence here emphasizes that government was instituted not to create rights, but to "secure" rights. As Jefferson explained on another occasion, "it is to secure our just rights that we resort to government at all."[1] The word "secure" is not used here in the sense of "obtain" or "procure," but means "to make secure," to safeguard, to protect, to preserve, to guarantee. Thus a mortgage may be given to "secure" a pre-existing debt.

The rights protected by the establishment of government are regarded as pre-existing; they antedate the existence of the government, and are not derived from it; on the contrary, their source is to be found in another place, and government is merely utilized as a suitable means or instrumentality in order to safeguard them more effectually than would be possible in the absence of politically organized society.

When speaking of "these" rights (namely, certain inalienable rights with which all human beings are endowed by their Creator, among which are life, liberty, and the pursuit of happiness), Jefferson is plainly referring to the "natural rights" which would be enjoyed in a "state of nature" in the absence of government. He is saying that nature dictates and reason requires, quite apart from the existence of any political institutions, that every person born into the world is entitled to the enjoyment of these rights.

In so doing, Jefferson is following Locke's view of the "state of nature" rather than that of Hobbes. Locke writes:

[15] 13 Stat. 48. See also 13 Stat. 31 (Nevada), 18 Stat. 474 (Colorado), 25 Stat. 677 (North Dakota, South Dakota, Montana, Washington), 28 Stat. 108 (Utah), 36 Stat. 558 (New Mexico), 36 Stat. 569 (Arizona). The act of April 30, 1802, 2 Stat. 174, for the admission of Ohio provides that its constitution shall not be repugnant to the ordinance of 1787. The act of February 20, 1811, 2 Stat. 642, for the admission of Louisiana, requires that its constitution "shall contain the fundamental principles of civil and religious liberty."

[1] *Works*, VIII, 165. Cf. *Hague* v. *C.I.O.*, 307 U. S. 496, 527 (1939).

The state of Nature has a law of Nature to govern it, which obliges every one, and reason, which is that law, teaches all mankind who will but consult it, that being all equal and independent, no one ought to harm another in his life, health, liberty or possessions.[2]

In similar vein, Jefferson as secretary of state wrote to the minister of France, which was then at war with England, that the United States was in a state of peace with all the belligerent powers, quite apart from treaties, by the law of nature. "For by nature's law, man is at peace with man, till some aggression is committed, which, by the same law, authorizes one to destroy another as his enemy."[3]

The "state of nature," according to Locke, is not to be confused with the state of war. The former exists when men are "living together according to reason without a common superior on earth, with authority to judge between them"; the latter occurs whenever there is "force without right." Hence "using force upon the people, without authority, and contrary to the trust put in him that does so, is a state of war with the people," and "the true remedy of force without authority is to oppose force to it." The people may resist those who use unjust force; the king's command will not excuse transgressions of the limitations of the law. "For the king's authority being given him only by the law, he cannot empower anyone to act against the law." It is not the people, but their unjust rulers who are guilty of rebellion. "For rebellion being an opposition, not to persons but to authority, which is founded only in the constitutions and laws of the government . . . those who set up force again in opposition to the laws do *rebellare*—that is, bring back again the state of war."[4]

But where such a common superior exists, the state of nature is superseded by civil society.

Those who are united into one body, and have a common established law and judicature to appeal to, with authority to decide

[2] *Two Treatises of Government*, 119.

[3] *Works*, VII, 400.

[4] *Two Treatises of Government*, 126–27, 195–96, 221, 231–32.

controversies between them and punish offenders, are in civil society with one another; but those who have no such common appéal, I mean on earth, are still in the state of Nature, each being where there is no other, judge for himself and executioner; which is, as I have before showed it, the perfect state of Nature.[5]

Hobbes, on the other hand, regarded the life of man in the state of nature as "solitary, poore, nasty, brutish, and short." It is a state of war "of every man against every man." In consequence "nothing can be Unjust. The notions of Right and Wrong, Justice and Injustice have there no place. Where there is no common Power there is no Law: where no Law, no Injustice." Likewise, property does not exist. Every man takes all "that he can get; and for so long, as he can keep it."[6]

Since "Covenants, without the Sword, are but Words, and of no strength to secure a man at all," it is necessary to erect a common power, to which each member of the society gives up his right of self-government on condition that the others do likewise. "This done, the Multitude so united in one Person, is called a COMMON-WEALTH, in latine CIVITAS. This is the Generation of that great LEVIATHAN, or rather (to speak more reverently) of that *Mortall God*, to which wee owe under the *Immortall God*, our peace and defence." The bearer of this indivisible authority is the sovereign.[7] According to Hobbes, the social compact is a covenant entered into by the people among themselves, and not a covenant between the people and the sovereign. Hence the ruler can never be guilty of breach of contract, releasing the people from their subjection.[8]

The doctrines of Hobbes became the foundation of the analytical school of jurisprudence. His *Leviathan*, published in 1651, justified royalists who had yielded to Parliament after the king's cause seemed hopeless. It did not please the thoroughgoing adherents of divine right. Locke's *Two Treatises* in defense of the "glorious revolution" which placed William and Mary upon the

[5] *Ibid.*, 159.
[6] Thomas Hobbes, *Leviathan*, 64–66.
[7] *Ibid.*, 87, 89–90, 95.
[8] *Ibid.*, 91.

throne appeared in 1690. Locke was obviously the guiding star followed by Americans when they patterned their revolution upon the English precedents of less than a century before.

Jefferson's agreement with Locke's view that natural rights existed in the absence of government is further shown by his statement that he would prefer newspapers without government to government without newspapers, and by his belief that the best form of polity was that of the Indians, where government was well-nigh nonexistent.[9]

That Jefferson rejected the opinion of Hobbes regarding the state of nature as a state of war "of every man against every man" is likewise plain. In describing the effects of taxation so severe that the people "have no sensibilities left but for sinning and suffering," Jefferson said, "Then begins, indeed, the *bellum omnium in omnia*, which some philosophers observing to be so general in this world, have mistaken it for the natural, instead of the abusive state of man."[10]

instituted among Men

That is, government is a human contrivance, not a divine institution. Medieval thinkers regarded law as an immutable system. The idea of legislation as a voluntary process was unfamiliar to them.[1] The king was an organ executing divine law, or the precepts of Roman law received as "written reason" (*ratio scripta*). Modern jurists recognize, just as Jefferson did,[2] that law can and must change. "The time has gone by when law is only an unconscious embodiment of the general will. It has become a conscious reaction upon itself of organized society seeking to determine its own destinies."[3] In the words of an eminent English thinker of Jefferson's time, "A government is, or ought to be,

[9] Jefferson, *Works*, V, 253, 255.

[10] *Ibid.*, XII, 11.

[1] Edward Dumbauld, "Dissenting Opinions in International Adjudication," *University of Pennsylvania Law Review*, Vol. XC, No. 8 (June, 1942), 930; John Dickinson, *Administrative Justice and the Supremacy of Law in the United States*, 85–86, 92, 101.

[2] Jefferson declared that "laws and institutions must go hand in hand with the progress of the human mind." *Works*, XII, 12.

[3] Holmes, *Collected Legal Papers*, 129–30.

GRAFF HOUSE

where the Declaration of Independence was written

nothing but an institution for collecting and carrying into execution the will of the people."[4]

deriving their just Powers

It has been said that "deriving" is the most important word in the Declaration.[1] For it shows that government is derivative, and possesses no inherent powers directly bestowed by divine ordinance upon rulers.

In *The Tenure of Kings and Magistrates*, John Milton regarded it as "manifest that the power of Kings and Magistrates is nothing else, but what is only derivative, transferred and committed to them in trust from the People, to the common good of them all, in whom the power yet remains fundamentally, and cannot be taken from them, without a violation of their natural birthright."[2]

Those who had believed in the divine right of kings did not admit that all just powers were derived from the consent of the people governed. They claimed that it was sin for the people under any circumstances to resist their rulers, because the powers of the government were God-given. Rebellion was therefore disobedience to God. Later it was learned that God could speak through the people as well as through kings. This was expressed in the maxim *Vox populi, vox Dei*. Contradicting the tenets of passive obedience, the democratic philosophy proclaimed, in words which Jefferson adopted as his motto, that "Rebellion to tyrants is obedience to God."[3]

While president of the United States, Jefferson wrote that "the will of the people . . . is the only legitimate foundation of any government."[4] More than two decades later, he criticized the English historian Hume, "the great apostle of Toryism," for denying the principle asserted by the House of Commons that the people are the origin of all just power: "And where else will

4 Richard Price, *Observations on the Nature of Civil Liberty*, 87.

1 McLaughlin, *A Constitutional History of the United States*, 103.

2 *The Works of John Milton*, V, 10 (spelling modernized).

3 Dumas Malone, *Jefferson the Virginian*, 242; Jefferson, *Writings*, XV, 415; Jefferson, *Papers*, I, 677–79.

4 *Writings*, X, 236.

this degenerate son of science, this traitor to his fellow men, find the origin of *just* powers, if not in the majority of the society? Will it be in the minority? Or in an individual of that minority?"[5]

But mere recognition that all political authority is held by delegation from the people does not ensure free government. There must be limits placed upon the powers delegated if they are to be "just powers." If delegation is absolute and unlimited, democracy becomes a fiction. The Byzantine absolutism of the Roman Empire was based theoretically upon the power of the people, which had been transferred to the emperor by the *lex regia*.[6] It may be conceded that, as Bracton says of the English king,[7] it is the law which is the source of all his royal powers; yet if that law makes those powers so great that the citizens in fact have no rights which the ruler is bound to respect, it is of little comfort to them to know that the king's powers are not God-given but derived from the people in accordance with law.[8] As expressed in an early Chinese poem,[9] to farmers toiling in the field every day from sunrise to sunset it does not matter much what the character of their government may be.

Besides a share in the public power, it is essential to good government that every citizen also possess substantial private rights

[5] *Ibid.*, XVI, 44. See page 33 above. The resolution of January 4, 1649, in connection with the trial of Charles I, declared "That the People under God are the Original of all just Powers." Hence "whatsoever is enacted . . . by the Commons . . . hath the force of Law . . . although the consent . . . of the King and House of Peers be not had thereunto." Rushworth, *Historical Collections*, VII, 1383.

[6] Justinian's codification contains the well-known statement of the jurist Ulpian: "*Quod principi placuit, legis habet vigorem: utpote cum lege regia, quae de imperio eius lata est, populus ei in eum omne suum imperium et potestatem conferat.*" ("The prince's pleasure has the force of law, since by the *lex regia* which was enacted concerning his sovereignty the people has conferred upon him all its sovereignty and power.") Dig. 1, 4, 1, pr. See also Inst. 1, 2, 6.

[7] "*Ipse autem rex non debet esse sub homine sed sub deo et lege, quia lex facit regem.*" ("For the king ought not be under any man, but under God and the law, since the law makes him king.") Bracton, *De legibus et consuetudinibus Angliae*, II, 33.

[8] Joseph Priestley, *An Essay on the First Principles of Government, and on the Nature of Political, Civil and Religious Liberty*, 48–50; Price, *Observations on the Nature of Civil Liberty*, 7.

[9] Herbert A. Giles, *A History of Chinese Literature*, 54.

upon which public authority does not encroach. In other words, both political liberty and civil liberty are vital features of a well-ordered society.[10] Political liberty without civil liberty would make each citizen a fractional part of a tyrant, but a total slave. As Jefferson angrily exclaimed regarding the defective Virginia Constitution after the Revolution: "An elective despotism was not the government we fought for."[11]

Civil liberty includes religious freedom, "the rights of thinking, speaking, forming and giving opinions, and perhaps all those which can be fully exercised by the individual without the aid of exterior assistance."[12] These are rights which it is useless or impossible to surrender to government, but which government is constantly tempted to invade, when an effectual bill of rights is lacking.[13] Jefferson regarded his authorship of the statute of Virginia for religious freedom as one of the three outstanding achievements of his life.[14]

the Consent of the Governed

Here the social-compact philosophy is proclaimed. In the state of nature, all men are free, living under the law of nature, without political society or government. Such society is created, and government established, by the agreement or consent of individuals to give up their natural liberty in exchange for a collective instrumentality to protect, more effectively than before, their most valuable natural rights, including life, liberty, and property. Such is the teaching of Locke's treatise on government, and such is the doctrine accepted by Jefferson as well as other American statesmen of the eighteenth century and here proclaimed in the Declaration of Independence.

[10] Priestley, *An Essay on the First Principles of Government*, 9, 48, 60.

[11] Ernest Barker (ed.), *Social Contract*, xlvi; Jefferson, *Works*, IV, 20. Cf. Stephen, *Horae Sabbaticae*, II, 12.

[12] Chinard, *Thomas Jefferson the Apostle of Americanism*, 81.

[13] Jefferson, *Works*, VI, 159.

[14] For this statute, see Hening, *The Statutes at Large*, Virginia, XII, 84–86; for Jefferson's draft, which was amended in the legislature, see Jefferson, *Works*, II, 438–41.

In Locke's view, "Men being, as has been said, by nature all free, equal, and independent, no one can be put out of this estate and subjected to the political power of another without his own consent." In another passage, Locke, citing Hooker, declares that the legislative power cannot be exercised except by "the hands where the community have once placed it . . . ; for without this, the law could not have that which is absolutely necessary to its being a law, the consent of the society, over whom nobody can have a power to make laws but by their own consent and by authority received from them."[1]

An emphatic affirmation that consent is "the true origin of the obligation of human laws" is found in Justice James Wilson's law lectures.[2] The Massachusetts House on March 2, 1773, in answer to a speech by Governor Hutchinson, asserted that "It is consent alone, that makes human laws binding," and quoted Locke and Hooker to the same effect.[3] John Dickinson in *An Essay on the Constitutional Power of Great Britain over the Colonies in America* declared in 1774 that "the freedom of a people consists in being governed by laws, in which no alteration can be made, without their consent."[4]

Today the social-contract theory is generally regarded as the embodiment of an obsolete mode of thinking. It is recognized as unhistorical,[5] as assuming the existence of conditions and events which are known never to have occurred. Of course, in America something very like the transactions postulated by the social-contract philosophy actually did occur. The Mayflower Compact, Colonial charters, and written constitutions for federal and state governments are examples of political authority specifically delegated by consent of the people governed. "The example of changing a constitution by assembling the wise men of the State, instead of assembling armies, will be worth as much to the world as the former examples we had given them," wrote Jefferson in 1789.[6]

[1] *Two Treatises of Government*, 164, 184.
[2] *The Works of the Honourable James Wilson*, I, 65, 71, 99, 200–205, 212, 218–20.
[3] *Massachusetts State Papers*, 387, 393, 395.
[4] *The Political Writings of John Dickinson*, I, 403.
[5] Gray, *The Nature and Sources of the Law* (2nd ed.), 72–74.
[6] *Works*, V, 469–70.

Organic or utilitarian philosophies have now become more popular, and the relationship between an individual and society is commonly regarded as an inevitable incident of human life, rather than as a status voluntarily created by the consent of persons free to choose whether or not they wish to abandon the "state of nature" and subject themselves to political authority.[7]

Yet the essential significance of the social-compact philosophy as an expression of ethical values is still vital and unquenchable. The Declaration of Independence did not say that, as a matter of historical fact, all governments derived their powers from the consent of the governed; it said that their *just* powers were so derived. It was not here speaking in terms of political history, but in terms of political justice. In this sense it is still a quite tenable belief, as it was long before the Fourth of July in the year of our Lord 1776, that "constitutional compact," or consent of the governed, was and is the only decent way of establishing political authority.[8]

The consent of the people through their representatives in Parliament was recognized in England from early times as an indispensable step in the enactment of laws. When King Edward I summoned Parliament in 1295, the writs began with a quotation from the Code of Justinian (Book 5, Title 58, Law 5: "*ut quod omnes similiter tangit ab omnibus approbetur*") "which was transmuted by Edward from a mere legal maxim into a great political and constitutional principle: 'As the most righteous law, established by the provident circumspection of the sacred princes, exhorts and ordains that that which touches all shall be approved by all, it is very evident that common dangers must be met by measures concerted in common.' " The right of the commons to participate in Parliament was thus recognized.[9]

Americans of the present generation do not find anything incredible or meaningless in the language of the Declaration that all just power is derived from the consent of the governed. A similar vitality and timeliness inheres in Jefferson's statement in

[7] Williams, *Chapters on Current International Law and the League of Nations*, 14; Percy W. Bridgman, *The Intelligent Individual and Society*, 166, 180, 272.

[8] McLaughlin, *The Foundations of American Constitutionalism*, 81.

[9] William Stubbs, *The Constitutional History of England* (4th ed.), II, 133.

1790 that "Every man, and every body of men on earth, possesses the right of self-government. They receive it with their being from the hand of nature."[10]

This traditional American principle of self-government was given world-wide application as an integral part of the war aims of the United States when it took up arms in 1917. In his message to Congress calling for a declaration of hostilities, President Wilson declared that "we shall fight for the things which we have always carried nearest our hearts, for democracy, for the right of those who submit to authority to have a voice in their own government, for the rights and liberties of small nations, for a universal dominion of right by such a concert of free peoples as shall bring peace and safety to all nations and make the world itself at last free." On a later occasion he said: "National aspirations must be respected; peoples may now be dominated and governed only by their own consent. 'Self-determination' is not a mere phrase. It is an imperative principle of action, which statesmen will henceforth ignore at their peril."[11]

Of course, as English critics of the Declaration observed, if it were necessary that the actual consent of every individual to each act done by the state be procured, it would paralyze the administration of public affairs. No one could be found guilty of violating any law, at least if he took the precaution of declaring his dissent before infringing it.[12] Practical necessities dictate that the principle of individual freedom must at least be tempered by majority rule and observance of plighted faith (*pacta sunt servanda*). But divine-right advocates may pertinently ask, How does a majority, in the absence of authority derived directly from God, obtain any rightful power over dissenting individuals in the minority? And if authority is derived directly from God, why may it not be conferred upon a single person (king or monarch) as effectively as upon a transient multitude? Jefferson's reply

[10] Jefferson, *Works*, VI, 98.

[11] Addresses to Congress, April 2, 1917, and February 11, 1918.

[12] John Lind, *An Answer to the Declaration of the American Congress*, 119, 120, 122, 126; [William Knox], *The Controversy between Great Britain and her Colonies Reviewed*, 88; John W. Gough, *The Social Contract*, 130; Dumbauld, "The Place of Philosophy in International Law," *University of Pennsylvania Law Review*, Vol. LXXXIII, No. 5 (March, 1935), 598.

would be that majority rule is "the natural law of every society," a "fundamental law of nature, by which alone self-government can be exercised." In his first inaugural address, he declared that "absolute acquiescence in the decisions of the majority" is "the vital principle of republics, from which is no appeal but to force, the vital principle and immediate parent of despotism." Where majority rule is not acknowledged, "there government ends, the law of the strongest takes its place, and life and property are his who can take them."[13]

Although the consent of the governed was in Jefferson's view the only legitimate basis for political authority, he recognized that this consent might be manifested in a variety of ways and through whatever agencies the people might establish for that purpose. "The whole body of the nation is the sovereign legislative, judiciary and executive power for itself. The inconvenience of meeting to exercise these powers in person, and their inaptitude to exercise them, induce them to appoint special organs to declare their legislative will, to judge & execute it. It is the will of the nation which makes the law obligatory; it is their will which creates or annihilates the organ which is to declare & announce it. They may do it by a single person, as an Emperor of Russia, (constituting his declarations evidence of their will,) or by a few persons, as the Aristocracy of Venice, or by a complication of councils, as in our former regal government, or our present republican one."[14]

Jefferson regarded government as republican only to the extent that popular participation in the political process was provided for. He considered it desirable that the people have a share in the enforcement of the laws (through the jury system), as well as in their enactment and in the election of the executive magistrate.[15] The same sentiment had been expressed by the youthful Sam Adams when Jefferson was a boy: "The two main provisions

[13] John W. Allen, *A History of Political Thought in the Sixteenth Century*, 385; John N. Figgis, *The Divine Right of Kings* (2nd ed.), 1, 261, 283–84; Hans Kelsen, *Allgemeine Staatslehre*, 370–71; Sir Dudley Digges, *The Unlawfulness of Subjects Taking up Arms against their Soveraigne, in what case soever*, 38; Jefferson, *Works*, VI, 98; IX, 106, 198; Jefferson, *Writings*, XVI, 337.
[14] *Works*, IX, 74.
[15] *Works*, XI, 527–33; XII, 4, 7; V, 483–84.

by which a certain share in the government is secured to the people are their Parliaments and their juries; by the former of which no laws can be made without their consent, and by the latter none can be executed without their judgment."[16] The chief grievance of which the Stamp Act Congress complained in 1765 was the British government's encroachment upon these two basic features of constitutional liberty.[17]

Jefferson believed "that government to be the strongest of which every man feels himself a part." Hence he regarded the American republic as "the strongest government on earth" where "every man at the call of the law would meet invasions of public order as his own personal concern."[18]

the Right of the People to . . . institute new Government

Perhaps as an outgrowth of the social-compact theory, it began to be perceived that if government was created by the consent of the people, it could doubtless with equal propriety and effect be re-created, or abolished, modified, and altered by them. What the people had given, the people could take away. The Declaration of Independence here asserts that the people may abolish an existing government at their pleasure and institute new government, of such kind and character as they deem desirable. This doctrine stands at the very opposite pole from that of writers such as Sir Dudley Digges, who denied the right of resistance against rulers in any case whatsoever.[1]

Digges, citing Calvin in support of the doctrine of nonresistance, holds that rebellion is sin. He considers monarchy the best and the "popular form the worst government." He draws an analogy between marriage and political society: "There are many resemblances in matrimony which will afford great light to the better understanding the duty of subjects. The consent of the woman makes such a man her husband, so the consent of the peo-

[16] Wells, *The Life and Public Services of Samuel Adams*, I, 21.
[17] Hezekiah Niles, *Principles and Acts of the Revolution in America*, 457, 460.
[18] *Works*, IX, 196; Dumbauld, *Thomas Jefferson, American Tourist*, 214.
[1] *The Unlawfulness of Subjects Taking up Arms against their Soveraigne, in what case soever*, 10, 37.

ple is now necessary to the making Kings (for conquest is a kinde of ravishing, which many times prepares the way to a wedding, as the Sabine women chosse [*sic*] rather to be wives, then [*sic*] concubines, & most people preferre the condition of subjects, though under hard laws to that of slaves.)" The view Digges censured "bestowes upon woman the breeches, as well as the crown upon the people, and . . . gives the same licence to women to cast off the bonds of Wedlock as to subjects those of subjection. As in marriage, so in Monarchy, . . . if it is once made the dissent of the inferior party . . . cannot dissolve the compact."[2]

The Declaration here recognizes the right of the people to alter their government whenever it has become destructive of the ends for which it was established, namely, to secure and safeguard their natural rights of life, liberty, and pursuit of happiness.

Does this mean that the government must invade or violate those basic rights before it can be removed? Must there be a breach of trust, as Locke required, before the "power of the people" can "take place"?[3] Must there be an infringement of the social contract before the people may oust their rulers?

Or do the people have the right to determine at any time that their government has become unsatisfactory, and is failing to achieve the purpose for which it was created? Is the government merely the agent of the people, which they may make and unmake as they see fit, and constitute or dissolve at their pleasure?

In *The Tenure of Kings and Magistrates,* the latter view was taken by John Milton, who declared "that since the King or Magistrate holds his authority of the people, both originally and naturally for their good in the first place, and not his own, then may the people as oft as they shall judge it for the best, either choose him or reject him, retain him or depose him though no Tyrant, merely by the liberty and right of free born Men, to be governed as seems to them best." Further on, he says: "Thus far hath been considered briefly the power of Kings and Magistrates; how it was originally the people's, and by them conferred in trust only to be employed to the common peace and benefit; with liber-

[2] *Ibid.*, 27, 129.
[3] *Two Treatises of Government,* 192–93: "this power of the people can never take place till the government be dissolved."

ty therefore and right remaining in them to reassume it to themselves, if by Kings or Magistrates it be abused; or so to dispose of it by any alteration, as they shall judge most conducing to the public good."[4]

Perhaps it does not really matter which of these alternatives be chosen, because, even under Locke's more restrictive criteria, "the people shall be judge" whether the government has violated its trust.[5] If the people are dissatisfied, they may well conclude that a breach of trust has occurred, even if the rulers have been dutiful and virtuous in their well-meant but ineffective efforts to promote the public welfare.

Locke enumerates five cases in which government is dissolved: where the ruler sets up his own arbitrary will in place of the laws; where he hinders the legislative power "from assembling in its due time or from acting freely"; where he alters the mode of electing the legislative representatives of the people; where he delivers the people into subjection to a foreign power; and where he abandons his trust and fails to put the laws in execution.[6] It will be noted that all but the fourth of these instances of dissolution of government are embodied in charges against George III in the Declaration of Independence; and perhaps the use of Hessian troops might even be regarded as delivering the people into the hands of a foreign power.

These events have the effect of altering the legislative power; and "When any one, or more, shall take upon them to make laws whom the people have not appointed so to do, they make laws without authority, which the people are not therefore bound to obey."[7] Government is also dissolved if the legislative or executive power should act contrary to their trust.

In these, and the like cases, Locke continues, in language which is echoed in the Declaration, "when the government is dissolved, the people are at liberty to provide for themselves by erecting a new legislative differing from the other by the change of persons, or form, or both, as they shall find it most for their

[4] *The Works of John Milton*, V, 14, 18 (spelling modernized).

[5] *Two Treatises of Government*, 241.

[6] *Ibid.*, 226–27.

[7] *Ibid.*, 225. The Declaration characterizes certain measures passed by Parliament as "acts of pretended legislation."

safety and good. . . . Whensoever, therefore, the legislative shall . . . endeavour to grasp themselves, or put into the hands of any other, an absolute power over the lives, liberties, and estates of the people, by this breach of trust they forfeit the power the people had put into their hands for quite contrary ends, and it devolves to the people, who have a right to resume their original liberty, and by the establishment of a new legislative (such as they shall think fit), provide for their own safety and security, which is the end for which they are in society."[8]

Even if the paragraph of the Declaration now under consideration has the same meaning as the above-quoted passages from Locke, it is plain that Jefferson's "felicity of expression" has notably improved the prosaic language of Locke. Here, as elsewhere in the Declaration, Jefferson's version possesses "the witchery of true substance wedded to perfect form." Only thus can one account for "the persistent fascination which this state-paper has had, and which it still has, for the American people, or for its undiminished power over them."[9]

But I venture to believe that Jefferson's statement of the scope of the people's power goes beyond Locke's doctrine, and permits the people at their pleasure to designate and to remove such agents as they choose for the transaction of their business and the administration of their affairs. At any rate, I believe that this is the sense in which the American people has interpreted and understood the Declaration. This is the philosophy which has animated the nation's political thinking and demanded that public officials be at all times the servants of the people, not their masters; that government be so constructed that as a matter of routine, rather than of revolution, it shall reflect the consent of the governed; that the will of the people shall be given effect in the daily operations of established agencies of administration, rather than required to have recourse to revolutionary violence when oppression and abuses shall have become intolerable.

[8] *Ibid.*, 228, 229. Locke explains that "What I have said here concerning the legislative in general holds true also concerning the supreme executor . . . when he goes about to set up his own arbitrary will as the law of the society." *Ibid.*, 229.

[9] Tyler, *The Literary History of the American Revolution*, I, 520.

This interpretation of the Declaration accords with other statements made by Jefferson regarding participation by the people in the process of government.

In his *Summary View of the Rights of British America* in 1774, he desired the King to reflect "that he is no more than the chief officer of the people, appointed by the laws, and circumscribed with definite powers, to assist in working the great machine of government, erected for their use, and consequently subject to their superintendance." A little later, as spokesman for "those who are asserting the rights of human nature," he declares: "They know, and will therefore say, that kings are the servants, not the proprietors of the people." In another passage Jefferson uses language more reminiscent of Locke's view: "From the nature of things, every society must at all times possess within itself the sovereign powers of legislation. . . . While those bodies are in existence to whom the people have delegated the powers of legislation, they alone possess and may exercise those powers; but when they are dissolved by the lopping off one or more of their branches, the power reverts to the people, who may exercise it to unlimited extent, either assembling together in person, sending deputies, or in any other way they may think proper."[10] With this should be compared the passage elsewhere in the Declaration stating that the legislative powers are "incapable of annihilation" and return to "the people at large for their exercise" when the executive prevents the ordinary legislature from meeting. In this contingency, Locke's doctrine also would permit exercise of legislative power by the people.

When the French monarchy was replaced by a republic, Jefferson was positive in maintaining that the new government should be recognized by the United States: "It accords with our principles to acknolege [*sic*] any government to be rightful which is formed by the will of the nation substantially declared." In justification of this position, he explained: "We surely cannot deny to any nation that right whereon our own government is founded, that every one may govern itself under whatever forms it pleases, and change these forms at it's own will. . . . The will of the nation is the only thing essential to be regarded." Developing the same

[10] Pages 5-6, 22, 19.

78

theme, he said: "I consider the people who constitute a society or nation as the source of all authority in that nation, as free to transact their common concerns by any agents they think proper, to change these agents individually, or the organization of them in form or function whenever they please."[11]

Recognition of the right of the people to transact their business through such agents as they please, and to change such agents at any time they see fit, is in substance recognition of the principle that political authority is a public trust and not a property right belonging to the ruler.

The public character of official powers was sometimes obscured by private law analogies. Thus in 1773 during the controversy between Governor Hutchinson of Massachusetts and the assembly, one of the arguments used in support of the local legislature's right to be free from interference by the Parliament in England was that otherwise the Massachusetts government would be deprived of its "property in the privileges granted to it" by the charter. In the answer of the Council, on February 25, 1773, to the Governor's speech of February 16, 1773, inferences are drawn from the Governor's previous admission that subordinate legislatures are permitted a place in the British constitution, although Parliament is the supreme authority. The Council insists that this implies that the authority granted to a subordinate legislature should be operative as far as the grant allows; and that, if the grantee does not exceed the limits prescribed in the grant, and if "no forfeiture be incurred," the supreme power cannot interfere with its functioning. "To suppose the contrary, is to suppose, that it has no property in the privileges granted to it; for, if it holds them at the will of the supreme power, which it must do, by the above supposition, it can have no property in them."[12] This argument that legislative power is a property right, a franchise or privilege granted to Massachusetts officeholders by the king, just as he might grant a piece of land by deed, exhibits a much less advanced theory of popular government than that deducible from the Declaration and from Jeffer-

---

11 *Works*, VII, 175, 198, 284–85. See also *ibid.*, IX, 74.
12 *Massachusetts State Papers*, 382.

son's statements regarding the right of the people at any time to modify their political system.

To be sure, in eighteenth-century England, public office was regarded generally as a species of private property. Commissions as officers in the army and navy were bought and sold as if they were merchandise. Some offices were hereditary, and descended to the heir of the holder just as landed estates descended. In more recent times the growth of "civil service" and the expansion of bureaucracy has revived the conception of public office as private property. When the tenure in office of public functionaries is protected by legislation which accords them a legal right to remain on the government pay roll, their status is substantially that of persons having "property in the privileges granted" to them of exercising governmental powers.

The people's right to govern themselves outweighs the right of any officeholder to govern them; public office cannot possibly be private property if governments derive all their just powers from the consent of the governed, and if the people are at liberty to choose new agents and to institute new government at any time they please to do so. For this reason, not only does no one have "a constitutional right to be a policeman," as Justice Holmes said,[13] but no one should have a property right to hold any public office whatsoever. A private right to serve the public is incompatible with the public's right to choose its own servants and to organize their powers in such form as the people shall deem "most likely to effect their safety and happiness."

In Jefferson's opinion it is as natural for a people to modify their government from time to time, so as to bring it into accord with current conditions, as it is for a boy to cast off child's clothing and put on new garments as he grows to manhood. "I am certainly not an advocate for frequent and untried changes in laws and constitutions. I think moderate imperfections had better be borne with; because, when once known, we accommodate ourselves to them, and find practical means of correcting their ill effects. But I know also that laws and constitutions must go hand in

[13] *McAuliffe* v. *New Bedford*, 155 Mass. 216, 220 (1892): "The petitioner may have a constitutional right to talk politics, but he has no constitutional right to be a policeman."

hand with the progress of the human mind. As that becomes more developed, more enlightened, as new discoveries are made, new truths disclosed, and manners and opinions change with the change of circumstances, institutions must advance also and keep pace with the times. We might as well require a man to wear still the coat which fitted him as a boy, as civilized society to remain ever under the regimen of their barbarous ancestors."[14]

But because of innate human conservatism, such changes will not be made unless necessitated by unendurable evils. Prudence will dictate, as the Declaration wisely states, that people are more disposed to suffer, while ills are sufferable, than to remedy the situation by drastic action. Thus it is a safe presumption that no government will ever be overthrown unless it deserves to be.[15] Unjustified rebellions or revolutions need not be feared.

If an uprising occurs because of misapprehension, when no real grievance actually exists, the remedy is to inform the people regarding the true state of affairs. It would show lack of public spirit if the people failed to revolt when they believed, however erroneously, that the government was guilty of tyrannical conduct. Hence the punishment for unsuccessful rebellions should never be too severe, lest the civic ardor of the people become apathetic. Abject and servile submission to unjust power should be discouraged, as being unworthy of freemen. In Jefferson's words:

> I hold it that a little rebellion now and then is a good thing, & as necessary in the political world as storms in the physical. Unsuccessful rebellions indeed generally establish the encroachments on the rights of the people which have produced them. An observation of this truth should render honest republican governors so mild in their punishment of rebellions as not to discourage them

[14] *Works*, XII, 11–12. Jefferson may have derived this analogy from Sir Matthew Hale. See Mark DeWolfe Howe, *Readings in American Legal History*, 98.

[15] Cf. Arthur Barnhart, "Princeton and the Problems of a Democracy," *Nassau Literary Magazine*, Vol. LXXIX (April, 1924), 369; Stephen, *Horae Sabbaticae*, II, 11.

too much. It is a medicine necessary for the sound health of government.[16]

When Shays' Rebellion in Massachusetts caused misgivings in Europe regarding the stability of American governments, Jefferson showed by a statistical computation that this was equivalent to approximately one rebellion for each state in a century and a half, since thirteen states had been independent for eleven years. He sagaciously inquired:

> What country before ever existed a century & half without a rebellion? & what country can preserve it's liberties if their rulers are not warned from time to time that their people preserve the spirit of resistance? Let them take arms. The remedy is to set them right as to facts, pardon & pacify them. What signify a few lives lost in a century or two? The tree of liberty must be refreshed from time to time with the blood of patriots & tyrants.[17]

Experimentation should not be discouraged, if the people are to perform properly their legitimate function of instituting new government, "laying its foundation on such principles, and organizing its powers in such form, as to them shall seem most likely to effect their safety and happiness."

more disposed to suffer

This expression appears in Locke, where it is said that "the people . . . are more disposed to suffer than right themselves by resistance."[1]

a long Train of Abuses

This expression appears in Locke. The English writer, refuting the assertion that recognition of the right of the people to alter their form of government would lead to frequent rebellion,

[16] *Works*, V, 256. The English writer Richard Price, whose thinking paralleled Jefferson's on many points, held a similar view. See his *Observations on the Nature of Civil Liberty*, 14.

[17] *Works*, V, 362. See also *ibid.*, 252–53, 263, 374.

[1] *Two Treatises of Government*, 233.

The Signing of the Declaration of Independence
from the Savage and Pine portrait

points out that "such revolutions happen not upon every little mismanagement in public affairs. . . . But if a long train of abuses, prevarications and artifices, all tending the same way, make the design visible to the people, . . . it is not to be wondered that they should then rouse themselves, and endeavour to put the rule into such hands which may secure to them the ends for which government was at first erected."[1]

The fact that the words "a long train of abuses" were followed in the Rough Draft by the phrase "begun at a distinguished period," which Congress omitted, shows that Jefferson was also drawing upon a passage in his *Summary View*: "Single acts of tyranny may be ascribed to the accidental opinion of a day; but a series of oppressions, begun at a distinguished period, and pursued unalterably through every change of ministers, too plainly prove a deliberate and systematical plan of reducing us to slavery."[2]

The History of the present King

It was during the reign of George III, which began in 1760, that the controversies between England and the Colonies became acute. On several occasions the colonists conceded that they would be contented if the state of things were restored which existed at the end of the Seven Years' War in 1763. Thus, the Continental Congress resolved on September 24, 1774, to confine its consideration of infringements of American rights to those occurring "since the year 1763," and in an address to the people of Great Britain on October 21, 1774, said: "Place us in the same situation that we were in at the close of the last war, and our former harmony will be restored."[1]

Ten years after independence had been declared, Jefferson summarized for a French historian the position taken by the colo-

[1] Locke, *Two Treatises of Government*, 231. Cf. *ibid.*, 223.
[2] Page 11.
[1] *Journals*, I, 42, 89. See also letter of the Massachusetts assembly to the Earl of Dartmouth, June 29, 1773, *Massachusetts State Papers*, 399; James Macpherson, *The Rights of Great Britain Asserted Against the Claims of America*, 16; Morison, *Sources and Documents illustrating the American Revolution*, 192, 194.

83

nists before the outbreak of the Revolution: "Let no new shackles be imposed, & we will continue to submit to the old. . . . Place us in the condition we were when the king came to the throne, let us rest so, & we will be satisfied. This was the ground on which all the states soon found themselves rallied, and that there was no other which could be defended."[2]

In his *Notes on Virginia*, Jefferson thus epitomizes the achievements of George III:

> It is unnecessary, however, to glean up the several instances of injury, as scattered through American and British history, and the more especially as, by passing on to the accession of the present king, we shall find specimens of them all, aggravated, multiplied and crouded within a small compass of time, so as to evince a fixed design of considering our rights natural, conventional and chartered as mere nullities. The following is an epitome of the first sixteen years of his reign. The colonies were taxed internally and externally; their essential interests sacrificed to individuals in Great Britain; their legislatures suspended; charters annulled; trials by juries taken away; their persons subjected to transportation across the Atlantic, and to trial before foreign judicatories; their supplications for redress thought beneath answer; themselves published as cowards in the councils of their mother country and courts of Europe; armed troops sent among them to enforce submission to these violences; and actual hostilities commenced against them. No alternative was presented but resistance, or unconditional submission. Between these could be no hesitation. . . . They declared themselves independent states.[3]

an absolute Tyranny

John Adams did not approve of the passages in the Declaration which called George III a tyrant. Writing to Timothy Pickering on August 6, 1822, he said: "There were other expressions which I would not have inserted had I drawn it up, particularly that which called the King tyrant. I thought this too personal; for

[2] *Works*, V, 189.
[3] *Ibid.*, IV, 16. See also *ibid.*, II, 71.

I never believed George to be a tyrant in disposition and in nature; I always believed him to be deceived by his courtiers on both sides of the Atlantic, and in his official capacity only cruel. I thought the expression too passionate, and too much like scolding, for so grave and solemn a document; but as Franklin and Sherman were to inspect it afterwards, I thought it would not become me to strike it out."[1] Jefferson doubtless used the term "tyrant" in the sense attributed to it by Locke and Milton, as meaning a ruler who exercises power without legal authority, to the detriment of the people.[2] In this sense, the charge of tyranny was fully established if the truth of the charges against the King set forth in the subsequent paragraphs of the Declaration was proved.[3]

Locke said that "tyranny is the exercise of power beyond right," and that "Wherever law ends, tyranny begins, if the law be transgressed to another's harm." He stressed the point that "whosoever in authority exceeds the power given him by the law, and makes use of the force he has under his command to compass that upon the subject which the law allows not, ceases in that to be a magistrate, and acting without authority may be opposed, as any other man who by force invades the right of another. This is acknowledged in subordinate magistrates. He that hath authority to seize my person in the street may be opposed as a thief and a robber if he endeavours to break into my house to execute a writ, notwithstanding that I know he has such a warrant and such a legal authority as will empower him to arrest one abroad. And why this should not hold in the highest, as well as in the most inferior magistrate, I would gladly be informed. . . . For exceeding the bounds of authority is no more a right in a great than a petty officer, no more justifiable in a king than a constable."[4]

In Milton's language, "A Tyrant . . . is he who regarding neither Law nor the common good, reigns only for himself and his faction."[5]

[1] *Works*, II, 514.

[2] McLaughlin, *A Constitutional History of the United States*, 102.

[3] Tyler, *The Literary History of the American Revolution*, I, 510–12; Herbert Friedenwald, *The Declaration of Independence*, 171. Cf. Hutchinson, *Strictures*, 30.

[4] *Two Treatises of Government*, 218, 219–20.

[5] *The Works of John Milton*, V, 18 (spelling modernized).

A similar understanding of the term appears in the charges against Charles I, for which he was put to death in 1649:

> That the said *Charles Stuart*, being admitted King of *England*, and therein trusted with a limited Power to govern by, and according to the Laws of the Land, and not otherwise; and by his Trust, Oath, and Office, being obliged to use the Power committed to him for the Good and Benefit of the People, and for the Preservation of their Rights and Liberties: yet nevertheless out of a wicked Design to erect and uphold in himself an unlimited and Tyrannical Power to rule according to his Will, and to overthrow the Rights and Liberties of the People, yea to take away and make void the Foundations thereof, and of all Redress and Remedy of Mis-government, which by the Fundamental Constitutions of this Kingdom were reserved on the Peoples behalf in the Right and Power of frequent and successive Parliaments, or National Meetings in Council: He the said *Charles Stuart*, for accomplishing of such his Designs, and for the Protecting of himself and his Adherents in his and their wicked Practices, to the same ends hath traitorously and maliciously levied War against the present Parliament and the People therein represented . . . .[6]

let Facts be submitted to a candid World

The following portion of the Declaration enumerates the specific grievances upon which the Colonies relied as their justification in the eyes of "a candid World" for their course in throwing off English rule. These "Injuries and Usurpations" are ordinarily less familiar and less interesting to Americans today than the general principles of government proclaimed in the second paragraph of the Declaration. But to contemporaries of Jefferson these charges had a definite, well-understood meaning and were directed against keenly felt grievances.[1]

[6] Rushworth, *Historical Collections*, VII, 1396.

[1] Sydney G. Fisher, "The Twenty-Eight Charges against the King in the Declaration of Independence," *Pennsylvania Magazine of History and Biography*, Vol. XXXI, No. 3 (July, 1907), 258.

The Charges Against the King

ABUSE OF EXECUTIVE POWER

H E has refused his Assent to Laws, the most wholesome
and necessary for the public Good.

This merely means that the King withheld his approval of
legislation enacted by Colonial assemblies. That prerogative had
been exercised by previous monarchs as well as by George III.
Indeed the Americans' theory of their relationship to England
was one of union only through the crown, and the King's failure
to veto certain "acts of pretended legislation" by Parliament is
urged in a subsequent part of the Declaration as a further grievance. Moreover, the royal veto power was recognized in the
fourth resolution of the declaration of rights adopted October 14,
1774, by the first Continental Congress and in Jefferson's *Summary View*.[1]

However, the veto power, where the king participates in
legislation, is to be distinguished from royal disallowance of
Colonial acts. The latter function was exercised through the Privy
Council and was regarded in England as an executive regulation, comparable to the issuance of instructions to governors.
Rhode Island, Connecticut, and Maryland were the only colonies which were not required to transmit their laws to England
for approval, and which hence did not experience the royal disallowance. The Carolinas and Jerseys had not been subject to this
requirement until they became royal provinces. Massachusetts
transmitted its laws regularly after 1691. Pennsylvania was
obliged to do so from the beginning.[2]

Although the King's action in disallowing Colonial legislation
can hardly be considered illegal or unconstitutional, it may well

[1] Lind, *An Answer to the Declaration*, 14; Jefferson, *Summary View*, 16.
[2] Charles M. Andrews, "The Royal Disallowance," *Proceedings of the
American Antiquarian Society*, Vol. XXIV (new series), Part 2 (October, 1914),
343, 345.

be regarded as unwise and adverse to "the public Good." In any event, it antagonized public sentiment in the Colonies.

Not only was disallowance of Colonial laws a grievance in itself, which gave rise to the passage in the Declaration here under consideration, but also it was a contributing factor which aggravated other grievances specified elsewhere in the Declaration. Thus acts were disallowed which dealt with creation of new counties, establishment of courts, tenure of judges, naturalization, and immigration.[3]

Analysis of cases in which the British government disallowed Colonial acts indicates that it followed a policy of striking down any laws which might be thought detrimental to the trade, navigation, profits, or other economic advantages of British merchants and property owners, as well as any laws which might be thought to infringe upon the political prerogatives of the crown.[4] Although the number of acts disallowed was only a small fraction of those passed by Colonial legislatures, yet a substantial number of laws failed to survive scrutiny in London. Thus, in the year 1776, twenty important Colonial statutes were stricken down.[5] Moreover, the prospect of rejection by a distant and unsympathetic bureaucracy of laws enacted by representatives of the people familiar with local problems and responsive to local needs hung over American legislatures like a sword of Damocles and was a source of constant irritation and uneasiness. Furthermore, the types of laws which England was most certain to disallow were precisely those to which the American public was most attached.

When Jefferson speaks in the Declaration of the disallowance of laws that were "the most wholesome and necessary for the public Good," he was doubtless restating the charge advanced in his *Summary View* that the British monarch had "rejected laws of the most salutary tendency."[6] Hence he probably had in mind, in

[3] See pages 94, 105, 108, and 112 below.
[4] For a good account of British methods and policies in passing upon American legislation, see Elmer B. Russell, *Review of American Colonial Legislation*, 109; and Andrews, "The Royal Disallowance," *Proceedings of the American Antiquarian Society*, Vol. XXIV (new series), Part 2 (October, 1914), 349.
[5] Friedenwald, *The Declaration of Independence*, 214.
[6] Page 16.

88

the later indictment of the King as in the earlier, the numerous occasions when attempts by the Colonies to abolish the slave trade had been repeatedly "defeated by his majesty's negative."[7] Imposition of prohibitive duties on the importation of slaves ran counter to the King's policy of protecting a profitable British trade from legislative interference. Though the Virginia House of Burgesses on April 1, 1772, petitioned the King to permit the Governor to assent to laws which would "check so very pernicious a Commerce," the British government refused to relax its instructions. These forbade laws detrimental to British commercial interests, and specifically commanded "that no Duty be laid on any Slave Imported payable by the Importer." The Virginia law of April 11, 1772, was disallowed in England, just as earlier efforts to curb the slave trade, made by Virginia and by other colonies, had met the same fate.[8]

A similar policy led to disallowance of laws to prevent the importation of convicts, indigent or infirm persons, and other undesirable immigrants. On the other hand, laws for the naturalization of acceptable immigrants were also disapproved by the British government, on the ground that they infringed upon powers belonging to the crown and Parliament. Another policy of the home government which ran counter to American public opinion was that against paper money. Because of the lack of specie, emission of bills of credit was universally desired throughout the Colonies, but was rarely permitted and then only in case of extreme necessity. For instance, grants to the crown to support military expeditions against the French and Indians were financed by issuance of paper certificates. Normally, creditors in England were carefully protected at the expense of debtors in America.

[7] *Works*, II, 79, 211. See page 174 below. Not all supporters of these laws may have been as public spirited as Jefferson. Some of the old settlers who had bred slaves wished to sell them at a high price to smaller farmers, without competition from importers. *Journals of the House of Burgesses of Virginia 1758–1761*, 284.

[8] *Journals of the House of Burgesses of Virginia 1770–1772*, 256–57, 283–84. On the act of April 11, 1772 (Hening, *The Statutes at Large*, Virginia, VIII, 530), see *ibid.*, 263, 315. It was disallowed on April 7, 1773. *Acts of the Privy Council*, V, 362–63. Regarding the instructions, see *ibid.*, IV, 210, V, 288; and Elizabeth Donnan (ed.), *Documents . . . of the Slave Trade*, III, 449, IV, 135.

Besides these widely experienced grievances,[9] there were other particular instances of disallowance which made a deep impression upon public sentiment in the Colonies. One such case was the disallowance of the Massachusetts act of December 6, 1766, pardoning the Stamp Act rioters and compensating the sufferers. The King by order in council of May 13, 1767, rejected that act, as being an encroachment upon the royal prerogative of granting pardons, and required enactment of a compensation law "unmixed with other matter whatsoever."[10]

On another occasion Virginia was profoundly shocked when the disallowance of a number of important acts necessitated publication of a revised version of the laws in force, and led to a remonstrance to the King by the assembly. This occurred in connection with the revisal of Virginia laws adopted at the October, 1748, session of the legislature. On April 8, 1752, the assembly learned from Lieutenant Governor Dinwiddie that on October 1, 1751, a substantial and vital portion of this codification had been disallowed by the King. Ten statutes had been rejected, and fifty-seven were confirmed.[11] Confirmation by the crown meant that no modification or repeal of those laws could be made by the assembly without special permission from the king, while reenactment of a law which had once been disallowed was also forbidden by the royal instructions to Colonial governors. Among the ten disapproved laws was an act for the establishment of the General Court. The very next day after the disallowance became known, a law was enacted to validate the proceedings of the General Court during the period between the date when the rejected law took effect and the date when it was disallowed.[12] Soon afterwards, on April 15, 1752, in an address to the King, the assembly

[9] Friedenwald, *The Declaration of Independence*, 215–18. In Pennsylvania, for example, disallowance of each of these types of laws had been experienced. *The Statutes at Large of Pennsylvania*, II, 455, 492 (naturalization); III, 520–21, V, 654–55, 711–16 (paper money); IV, 503–504 (convicts); *Acts of the Privy Council*, V, 398 (slave trade).

[10] John Almon, *A Collection of Interesting and Authentic Papers, relative to the Dispute between Great Britain and America*, 135–42 (hereafter cited as Almon, *Prior Documents*); *Acts of the Privy Council*, V, 87–88.

[11] *Acts of the Privy Council*, IV, 140.

[12] See page 112 below.

protested against the action of the crown, and undertook to justify all but two of the laws disallowed.[13]

In 1752, William Hunter at Williamsburg printed *The Acts of Assembly, Now in Force, in the Colony of Virginia*. George Wythe's name appears in the list of subscribers, and Edmund Pendleton's copy of the book is in the Huntington Library. This collection included the ten laws disallowed. In 1753 the same printer issued a new volume, *Acts of Assembly, Now in Force in Virginia. Occasioned by the Repeal of Sundry Acts Made in the Twenty Second Year of His Majesty's Reign, and in the Year of Our Lord 1748*. This contained twenty laws revived by the repeal of the acts of 1748. The disallowed acts were omitted in the last edition of Virginia laws before the Revolution, printed in 1769, which is often cited as the "Old Body of Laws."[14]

HE *has forbidden his Governors to pass Laws of immediate and pressing Importance, unless suspended in their Operation till his Assent should be obtained; and when so suspended, he has utterly neglected to attend to them.*

The practice of requiring a suspending clause when certain types of laws were enacted began during the reign of Queen Anne. A royal circular letter of November 8, 1708, to Colonial governors first imposed that requirement as the result of an act which had been passed in the Barbados, enabling debts to be paid with paper money to the detriment of English merchants. The customary wording of the instruction regarding a suspending clause made it applicable to "extraordinary" laws, particularly those which affected trade, navigation, or other British economic interests, and those which infringed upon the political prerogative of the crown.[1] These were precisely the subjects which were apt to give rise to disputes between England and the Colonies.

[13] Hening, *The Statutes at Large*, Virginia, V, *iv*, 432–44, 567–68.

[14] See William H. Martin, "Some Virginia Law Books in a Virginia Law Office," *Virginia Law Register* (new series), Vol. XII, No. 6 (October, 1926), 322–30.

[1] Lind, *An Answer to the Declaration*, 16; Leonard W. Labaree, *Royal Instructions*, I, 142; "Instructions to Lord Dunmore," in *Aspinwall Papers*, Part II, *Collections of the Massachusetts Historical Society* (4th series), 637–38.

Parliament had impliedly sanctioned the practice of insisting upon suspending clauses. On April 25, 1740, in connection with resolutions regarding the rate of exchange for foreign money in the Colonies and the issuance of bills of credit under the authority of Colonial laws, Parliament presented an address to the King requesting "That he will be graciously pleased to require and command the respective Governors of his Colonies and Plantations in *America,* punctually and effectively to observe his Majesty's Royal Instructions, not to give Assent to, or to pass, any Act, whereby Bills of Credit may be issued in lieu of Money, without a Clause be inserted in such Act, declaring That the same shall not take effect until the said Act shall be approved by his Majesty."[2]

Royal instructions were formulated on March 12, 1752, for issuance to Colonial governors directing them "forthwith to consider and revise all and every the laws statutes and ordinances which are in force," except those of a private nature, "and in lieu thereof frame & pass a complete and well digested body of new laws, taking especial care that in the passing of each law, due regard be had to the methods and regulations prescribed by our instructions to you, and that no law of any kind whatever, making a part of such new body of laws, be passed without a clause be inserted therein, suspending & deferring the execution thereof untill our royall will & pleasure may be known thereupon." Each law was to be transmitted separately "together with very particular observations thereon" to the Lords Commissioners for Trade and Plantations, to be laid before the Privy Council "for our approbation or disallowance."[3] Virginia petitioned without avail in the same year to be relieved from the requirement of a suspending clause.[4]

In Jefferson's *Summary View,* he charged that the King permitted Colonial legislation to lie neglected in England for years

[2] Lind, *An Answer to the Declaration,* 20; *Journals of the House of Commons,* XXIII, 528. On April 28, 1740, Parliament was informed that the King had stated that he would give directions accordingly.

[3] *Documents Relative to the Colonial History of the State of New-York,* VI, 754–56.

[4] Andrews, "The Royal Disallowance," *Proceedings of the American Antiquarian Society,* Vol. XXIV (new series), Part II (October, 1914), 361.

without attention. "With equal inattention to the necessities of his people here has his majesty permitted our laws to lie neglected in England for years, neither confirming them by his assent, nor annulling them by his negative; so that such of them as have no suspending clause we hold on the most precarious of all tenures, his majesty's will, and such of them as suspend themselves till his majesty's assent be obtained, we have feared, might be called into existence at some future and distant period, when time, and change of circumstances, shall have rendered them destructive to his people here. And to render this grievance still more oppressive, his majesty by his instructions has laid his governors under such restrictions that they can pass no law of any moment unless it have such suspending clause; so that, however immediate may be the call for legislative interposition, the law cannot be executed till it has twice crossed the atlantic, by which time the evil may have spent its whole force."[5]

Such "neglect" was in many cases doubtless a polite mode of withholding assent. In other instances it was a consequence of the manner in which a gentlemanly, easygoing bureaucracy operated. In 1770, four Virginia laws were enacted which were not considered by the Lords Commissioners for Trade and Plantations until three years later, when one of them was suspended for further study.[6] A striking instance of delay occurred in North Carolina, where Governor Josiah Martin wrote to the English government on May 5, 1774, urging ratification of a law enacted twenty years before.[7]

He *has refused to pass other Laws for the Accommodation of large Districts of People, unless those People would*

[5] Page 17. Governors were forbidden by their standing instructions to assent without special permission to acts altering or repealing a law confirmed by the crown. Whether confirmed or not, an existing law could not be modified except by an act containing a suspending clause. "Instructions to Lord Dunmore," in *Aspinwall Papers*, Part II, *Collections of the Massachusetts Historical Society* (4th series), 637. Relief from this requirement had been sought in vain by Massachusetts and Virginia. *Acts of the Privy Council*, III, 676; V, 164; Labaree, *Royal Instructions*, I, 128-31.

[6] Lind, *An Answer to the Declaration*, 22; Friedenwald, *The Declaration of Independence*, 220.

[7] *The Colonial Records of North Carolina*, IX, 991-92.

relinquish the Right of Representation in the Legislature, a Right inestimable to them, and formidable to Tyrants only.

This charge refers to the refusal of permission to create new counties, towns, townships, or other incorporated communities, unless they would forego their right to representation in the assembly.

Massachusetts experienced this grievance. By the charter of that colony "each of the said Towns and Places" was empowered "to elect and depute Two Persons, and no more, to serve for and represent them respectively" in the "Great and General Court or Assembly." To this body was given "full Power and Authority, from time to time, to direct, appoint, and declare what Number each County, Town, and Place shall elect and depute to serve for, and represent them respectively." By an act passed in 1692 and confirmed by the crown on August 2, 1695, it was directed that Boston should send four; other towns of 120 or more freeholders, two; those of 40 or more, one; while those of 30 to 40 might send one or not as they wished; and those of less than 30 might send one or join with a neighboring district upon paying a proportionate part of the expense entailed. Thus, as new towns were formed, the membership of the assembly increased from 84 at the time of the charter to over 180, while that of the council remained fixed at 28.

This increase in the numbers and influence of the popular branch of the legislature was thought "inconvenient" and disadvantageous to the interests of the crown. Hence when Governor William Shirley's letter of October 18, 1742, brought the situation to the attention of the British government, instructions were issued which prevented the establishment of any new communities unless they would relinquish their right to representation in the legislature. The crown believed that "any further settlements may be erected into precincts, parishes, or villages, with all the officers necessary for their good government and security without the liberty of sending representatives to the general assembly."

This particular mode of diminishing the share of the people in government was so clearly contrary to the charter that it was abandoned in 1761. When the accession of George III to the throne occasioned the issuance of a new commission and instructions to the governor in that year, the former Article 48 concerning the erection of new towns was omitted. The English authorities conceded that it was not "consistent with the Constitution for the Crown to restrain by Instruction to the Governor, the exercise of those Powers which are Vested in the Legislature there by express words in the Charter and by a Law confirmed so long since as the Year 1692 and acted under ever since." Hence in 1767 eighteen Massachusetts laws for creation of new townships were allowed to "lie by" unrepealed, while new methods were sought for curtailing the people's power in that colony. Acts of the same sort, however, which had been passed in New Hampshire, South Carolina, and New York on May 9, 1764, August 9, 1765, and July 3, 1766, respectively, were disallowed on June 26, 1767, by the King in council. Virginia also lacked the protection which Massachusetts derived from the special provisions of its charter, and remained subject to the general instruction prohibiting the establishment of new counties unless the acts of assembly by virtue of which they were formed contained no provision regarding representation in the legislature.[1]

In his *Summary View* Jefferson forcefully stated this grievance:

But in what terms, reconcileable to majesty, and at the same time to truth, shall we speak of a late instruction to his majesty's governor of the colony of Virginia, by which he is forbidden to assent to any law for the division of a county, unless the new county will consent to have no representative in assembly? That colony has as yet fixed no boundary to the westward. Their western counties, therefore, are of indefinite extent; some of them are actually seated many hundred miles from their eastern limits. Is it possible,

[1] *Acts and Laws* of Massachusetts, *x*, 34; Hutchinson, *Strictures*, 12; Lind, *An Answer to the Declaration*, 25–28; Russell, *Review of American Colonial Legislation*, 186–87; Labaree, *Royal Instructions*, I, 111; *Acts and Resolves* of Massachusetts, III, 70–72; *Acts of the Privy Council*, IV, 475–76; V, 29–30, 32–34, 35, 40; "Instructions to Lord Dunmore" [February 11, 1771], in *Aspinwall Papers*, Part II, *Collections of the Massachusetts Historical Society* (4th series), 635–36.

then, that his majesty can have bestowed a single thought on the situation of those people, who, in order to obtain justice for injuries, however great or small, must, by the laws of that colony, attend their county court, at such a distance, with all their witnesses, monthly, till their litigation be determined? Or does his majesty seriously wish, and publish it to the world, that his subjects should give up the glorious right of representation, with all the benefits derived from that, and submit themselves the absolute slaves of his sovereign will? Or is it rather meant to confine the legislative body to their present numbers, that they may be the cheaper bargain whenever they shall become worth a purchase.[2]

The increase of such local government units is properly described in the Declaration as being "for the Accommodation of large Districts of People" because the difficulties of transportation in the eighteenth century made it highly inconvenient to attend distant county seats. The Journal of the Virginia assembly shows frequent instances of bills for division of counties, and Jefferson served on committees to which such requests for partition were referred.[3]

Though sometimes conceding that a particular area deserved representation, the British government insistently maintained that this privilege was one that must be granted by the king in the exercise of his royal prerogative and not by legislative enactments in which the people had a voice. Such a policy inevitably aroused resentment and antagonism. To people nurtured in traditions of liberty and believing that it was their birthright "to be governed by no Laws but what are of their own making; that is, such as they have assented to," it was obvious that interference by the crown in the selection of the popular branch of the legislature impaired the integrity of the constitutional processes. Very naturally a vigorous clamor arose in North Carolina when Governor George Burrington, without legislative sanction, issued writs for election of members of the assembly from precincts previously unrepresented:

[2] Pages 17–18.

[3] During Jefferson's first year in the House of Burgesses, several such requests were presented. *Journals of the House of Burgesses of Virginia 1766–1769,* 267, 275, 279.

Does it not savour of absurdity to say that the People have a part in making their Laws, for that their Representatives are to advise, assent, and approve of them before they are made, but that the Governor and Council are entirely of themselves to say and direct what shall be the Representatives to give and declare such advice, assent and approbation; as if they may divide old and erect new Precincts at their pleasure in effect they will do. Will such be the Delegates of the People? Will the People have any part in enacting such laws? Will they not be the Laws of the Governor and Council? [4]

The House on July 7, 1733, voted not to admit the members from the new precincts. Provision was then made by statute for the establishment of new counties, and their representation in the legislature. [5] Later, however, the partisans of royal prerogative had their innings. A dozen acts for erecting towns and counties were repealed by the King on April 8, 1754, but were re-enacted by special permission in 1756. A similar bill was vetoed by Governor Josiah Martin on March 1, 1772, pursuant to his instructions of February 6, 1771. [6]

Soon after disallowance of the South Carolina law of August 9, 1765, for establishing a new parish, general instructions, which remained in force from 1767 until the Revolution, were issued to the governors of the Colonies on this subject:

Whereas laws have at several times been passed in many of our colonies and plantations in America by which certain parishes and districts have been empowered and authorized to send representatives to the general assemblies of the respective colonies in which the said parishes and districts lie, and sundry other regulations have been introduced by those laws relative to the said assemblies; it is our will and pleasure and we do hereby require and

[4] *The Colonial Records of North Carolina*, III, 451, 456. To use an analogy from present-day industrial relations, the crown's position resembled that of a company insisting that management must participate in the designation of labor representatives for collective bargaining.

[5] *Ibid.*, 574-76.

[6] *Ibid.*, V, 92, 151, 659, 687; VI, 228; VIII, 515; IX, 258. See also Labaree, *Royal Instructions*, I, 103-104.

command that you do not upon any pretense whatever give your assent to any law . . . by which the number of the assembly shall be enlarged or diminished, the duration of it ascertained, the qualification of the electors, or the elected fixed or altered, or by which any regulations shall be established with respect thereto, inconsistent with our instructions to you our governor as prejudicial to that right or authority which you derive from us in virtue of our royal commission and instructions.[7]

The Governor of New York was reminded of this policy in 1768 by his superiors in England, and was instructed that he might with propriety assent to an act for the division of Albany County "provided it is silent as to the Representation in the Assembly, which tho' it is certainly a privilege that ought not to be denied to the new County, yet His Majesty considers that this ought to be derived from his Royal Grace & favour, & therefore consents that you should (in case the Legislature think fit to create a new county) issue writs for the election of two Members to the General Assembly; but His Majesty does not approve of its being made a part of the Law."[8]

In New Hampshire the controversy continued intermittently for many years. On January 26, 1745, the assembly voted to deny the right to sit of five representatives elected pursuant to the king's writ, but not by virtue of any law of the colony authorizing their constituents to be represented. A sixth member was later refused admission for the same reason. Governor Benning Wentworth, after considerable altercation, permitted the assembly to proceed to business, on account of the exigencies of war with the

[7] Labaree, *Royal Instructions*, I, 107; *Documents Relating to the Colonial History of the State of New Jersey*, IX, 638-39; "Instructions to Lord Dunmore," in *Aspinwall Papers*, Part II, *Collections of the Massachusetts Historical Society* (4th series), 635-36; *Documents Relative to the Colonial History of the State of New-York*, VII, 946. The King's displeasure was signified when a New York act of January 27, 1770, excluding judges from being members of the assembly, was disallowed on June 6, 1770. *Ibid.*, VIII, 210; *Acts of the Privy Council*, V, 244. For other rejected laws affecting the New York assembly, see *ibid.*, II, 850; III, 617. For instances in New Jersey, South Carolina, and Virginia, see *ibid.*, III, 343-44; 568; IV, 49, 487; V, 286. Cf. *ibid.*, V, 283.

[8] *Documents Relative to the Colonial History of the State of New-York*, VIII, 81, 100. An earlier act of July 3, 1766, for the erection of Cumberland County had been disallowed on June 26, 1767. *Acts of the Privy Council*, V, 35.

The Declaration Chamber in Independence Hall

French and Indians, but soon dissolved it, on May 3, 1745, when it refused to appropriate funds for the support of Fort Dummer.[9]

The next assembly renewed the struggle when it met. It promptly excluded several members upon the same grounds as before. The Governor refused to approve the speaker chosen by the House as thus constituted. Thereupon the assembly vigorously denied that the Governor had power "to Negative a Speaker and Introduce Members amongst us not Warranted by Law Usage or Custom or any other Authority that we Can find." When a copy of a portion of an additional instruction of June 30, 1748, from the King to the Governor relating to the dispute of 1745 was exhibited by claimants in support of their right to sit, the assembly ignored that expression of the King's will, because it had not been transmitted to them by the Governor through official parliamentary channels. Other captious arguments were also advanced for disregarding it, while professing a dutiful desire to respect the King's pleasure. On February 16, 1749, the assembly voted that admission of the new members be suspended until his Majesty's pleasure be further known, and on April 7, 1749, adopted an address to the crown on the subject. This assembly was dissolved on January 4, 1752, having done no business, and quarreled continuously with the Governor for a period of three years.[10] A more pliant or prudent assembly which met in the autumn of 1752 yielded to the British view,[11] and the dispute remained dormant until 1775 when the authority of the crown was rapidly disappearing in America.

On June 13, 1775, the New Hampshire assembly refused to seat representatives from three towns who had been returned by virtue of the king's writ. On July 14, Governor John Wentworth urged the assembly to rescind that action. Justifying the exclusion of these members, the assembly on the same day answered that for the Governor to send writs to such towns as he might think proper, without concurrence of the other branches of the legislature, was a cruel and arbitrary stretch of prerogative, which in

[9] *Provincial Papers . . . of New-Hampshire* (edited by Nathaniel Bouton), V, 262, 264, 295.

[10] *Ibid.*, VI, 70–77, 82–93, 125.

[11] *Ibid.*, VI, 129, 138–39, 161, 840, 883; Russell, *Review of American Colonial Legislation*, 187.

effect would permit the crown to choose the representatives of the people.[12] The Governor's reply, dated the following day, reminded the assembly that they themselves had been elected in accordance with the same traditional procedure as the excluded members. This was his last message to the assembly before the Revolution put an end to British government in America.

HE *has called together Legislative Bodies at Places unusual, uncomfortable, and distant from the Depository of their public Records, for the sole Purpose of fatiguing them into Compliance with his Measures.*

This charge appears on a separate slip of paper which Jefferson pasted on the Rough Draft. Accordingly it may be surmised that the suggestion to include this grievance originated with John Adams, for the controversy on this subject between the Massachusetts assembly and the royal governors of that province was one of long standing.[1]

In 1769 there were British troops in Boston (a circumstance itself regarded as a grievance)[2] and Governor Francis Bernard, because of complaints that the assembly might be overawed by military power, summoned the lawmakers to meet in Cambridge, across the Charles River, where no soldiers were present. The dispute began when the House protested to Governor Bernard against the presence of armed forces on the day the Council was to be elected. The Governor replied that he had no authority over the King's ships or troops, and could not order their removal. But he removed the assembly to Cambridge.[3] After his return to England, the controversy was resumed with Lieutenant Governor Thomas Hutchinson. It was now claimed by the House that Cambridge was at a distance from their records.[4]

---

[12] *Provincial Papers . . . of New-Hampshire,* VII, 373, 378, 383–86; Force, *American Archives* (4th series), II, 1175, 1678–79.

[1] Becker, *The Declaration of Independence,* 155. In South Carolina, also, the assembly was summoned to meet at Beaufort in 1772.

[2] *Massachusetts State Papers,* 178.

[3] *Ibid.,* 166–72.

[4] *Ibid.,* 196, 206.

The point was also made that it was illegal to convene anywhere but in Boston.[5] On May 31, 1770, Hutchinson indicated his willingness to remove the assembly from Harvard College to any other part of Cambridge, if desired. A few months afterward he offered to go to any place except Boston. On November 16, 1770, the House adopted a resolution agreeing to do business in Cambridge because of the need to inquire into the legality of Hutchinson's turning over the garrison at Castle William to Lieutenant Colonel Dalrymple and to forestall attempts to vacate the Massachusetts charter.[6]

On April 5, 1771, two days after notifying the General Court of his appointment by the King as governor, Hutchinson declared that he could not permit a return to Boston so long as it was claimed by the assembly as a right. He did agree to seek permission for returning to Boston, but later professed inability to obtain such permission unless the assembly would admit the royal power to fix the place of meeting. On April 10, 1772, the House explicitly reaffirmed its former position, in order that no admission of such power might be implied from further petitions to return to Boston.[7] Otis and Hancock had wavered in the course of the controversy, but the intrepidity of Sam Adams finally prevailed, and on June 13, 1772, the assembly was adjourned to Boston.[8] On May 26, 1774, General Gage, who had succeeded Hutchinson as governor, announced that the assembly would meet at Salem until the King signified his pleasure to permit it to meet again in Boston.[9]

The same grievance was experienced in Virginia, while Jefferson was a member of the House of Burgesses. On June 8, 1775, Lord Dunmore announced to the House that he thought it dangerous to remain in the Palace and had taken refuge on a warship, the *Fowey*. On June 21, 1775, the House informed him that his absence impeded the public business and deprived them

[5] *Ibid.*, 199–200.

[6] *Ibid.*, 210, 258, 286–87.

[7] *Ibid.*, 296, 301, 314, 315, 324–25.

[8] Wells, *Life and Public Services of Samuel Adams*, I, 369, 393–96, 403, 465–66, 472–73, 477; James K. Hosmer, *Life of Thomas Hutchinson*, 211, 213, 225.

[9] *Massachusetts State Papers*, 413–17.

of their constitutional right of access. He replied the next day that the constitution gave him the power to summon the assembly to such place as he chose, and he invited them to his "present residence" for the purpose of giving his assent to pending legislation. The Burgesses made answer, on June 24, 1775, that it was a breach of the privileges of the House to be asked to assemble on board a warship.[10]

It seems likely that Jefferson had this incident in mind as well as the Massachusetts controversy, because a warship could more appropriately be regarded as an "unusual" and "uncomfortable" meeting place than could Harvard College.

HE *has dissolved Representative Houses repeatedly, for opposing with manly Firmness his Invasions on the Rights of the People.*

Jefferson recollected from personal experience the dissolution of the Virginia House of Burgesses in 1769, 1773, and 1774. On those occasions the members withdrew to the Apollo Room of the Raleigh Tavern in Williamsburg and continued their proceedings, without the Governor's official sanction.[1]

The General Court of Massachusetts, the "representative house" of that province, was likewise dissolved on several occasions. The most striking instance was in connection with the issuance of a circular letter on February 11, 1768, by that body to the legislatures of the other colonies, charging that American rights had been infringed by king and Parliament.[2] When this letter came to the attention of the British government, Lord Hillsborough wrote to Governor Bernard on April 22, 1768, requiring him to dissolve the General Court if the circular letter were not rescinded. Governors of other colonies had been instructed on the preceding day that "It is his Majesty's pleasure that you should, immediately upon the receipt hereof, exert your

[10] *Journals of the House of Burgesses of Virginia 1773–1776*, 206, 273, 276, 280–81.

[1] Dumbauld, *Thomas Jefferson, American Tourist*, 33.

[2] *Massachusetts State Papers*, 134–36.

utmost influence to defeat this flagitious attempt to disturb the public peace, by prevailing upon the assembly of your province to take no notice of it, which will be treating it with the contempt it deserves."[3]

Governor Bernard advised the House that if he dissolved the assembly, he would not call another until so commanded by the King. On June 30, 1768, the House by a vote of 92 to 17 resolved not to rescind the circular letter. The next day the General Court was dissolved.[4] The legislative bodies of South Carolina and Georgia were also dissolved for failing to treat the Massachusetts circular letter "with the contempt it deserves," as directed by Lord Hillsborough.

General Gage dissolved the Massachusetts assembly on June 17, 1774, for expressing the wish that his administration would be in contrast with those of his predecessors Bernard and Hutchinson. Gage considered this address "an insult to his Majesty, and the Lords of the Privy Council, and an affront to myself."[5] A revolutionary provincial congress was soon established by the people to transact the public business.

HE *has refused for a long Time, after such Dissolutions, to cause others to be elected; whereby the Legislative Powers, incapable of Annihilation, have returned to the People at large for their exercise; the State remaining in the mean time exposed to all the Dangers of Invasion from without, and Convulsions within.*

In Virginia and Massachusetts in 1774, extralegal conventions were held when the royal governors refused to summon the usual assembly.[1] In that year all but five colonies had to elect their delegates to the Continental Congress by conventions, because their usual assemblies had been dissolved. In 1768 a town meeting in Boston and a provincial congress in Massachusetts

---

[3] Almon, *Prior Documents*, 203–204, 220; *Journals*, I, 97; Wells, *Life and Public Services of Samuel Adams*, I, 179, 192.

[4] *Massachusetts State Papers*, 146–50.

[5] *Ibid.*, 415–16.

[1] Lind, *An Answer to the Declaration*, 35–36.

had been similarly convened.[2] On February 5, 1774, the Massachusetts House informed Governor Hutchinson that committees of correspondence were necessary because the sessions of the Colonial assemblies depended on the caprice of their governors.[3]

The assembly of North Carolina also emphasized that it was the right of the people to assemble in a peaceable and orderly manner to petition for redress of grievances, and that extra-constitutional conventions were necessary because of the precarious contingency upon which the assembly's meetings depended, namely, the pleasure of the crown.[4] Attempts on the part of the Governor to prevent meetings of the Continental Congress and similar bodies on the ground that they were unlawful assemblages drew from the freeholders of Pitt County on August 15, 1774, a resolution "that if the Constitutional Assembly of this Colony are prevented from exercising their rights of providing for the security of the liberties of the people, that right again reverts to the people as the foundation from whence all power and legislation flow."[5]

This resolution, like Jefferson's statement in the Declaration of Independence, adopts Locke's doctrine[6] that when the established government fails to function, the people resume the powers of direct action which they would have in a "state of nature" prior to the formation of government.[7]

The British government's request of January 4, 1775, that the governors of the Colonies make efforts to prevent the meeting of the second Continental Congress led Governor Martin of North Carolina to issue a proclamation for that purpose, when his council advised him that he had no power to do anything more effective.[8]

Mindful of these efforts of the royal government to prevent action by the people, the framers of the First Amendment to the Constitution of the United States provided in that article of the

[2] Wells, *Life and Public Services of Samuel Adams*, I, 213-18.

[3] *Massachusetts State Papers*, 411.

[4] *The Colonial Records of North Carolina*, IX, 1202. The Governor dissolved the assembly the next day after this address of April 7, 1775.

[5] *Ibid.*, 1028-30.

[6] *Two Treatises of Government*, 192-93, 228, 242.

[7] Jefferson, *Works*, I, 83; VI, 33.

[8] *The Colonial Records of North Carolina*, IX, 1108, 1177-78.

American bill of rights that "Congress shall make no law . . . abridging . . . the right of the people peaceably to assemble, and to petition the Government for a redress of grievances."

HE *has endeavoured to prevent the Population of these States; for that Purpose obstructing the Laws for Naturalization of Foreigners; refusing to pass others to encourage their Migrations hither, and raising the Conditions of new Appropriations of Lands.*

With reference to a prior charge against the King, it was mentioned that naturalization laws were among those of whose disallowance the colonists complained. A royal instruction of November 24, 1773, prohibited assent to naturalization acts,[1] though few had been approved since the proclamation of October 7, 1763, forbidding westward immigration beyond the Ohio River. New York, New Jersey, Virginia, Pennsylvania, and North Carolina experienced the detrimental effects of this grievance.[2]

Disallowance of a North Carolina act of January 15, 1771, exempting certain immigrants from taxes for four years, gave rise to the charge that the King was refusing to pass laws for encouraging the migration of foreigners to the Colonies. This act was disallowed on April 22, 1772. The English government feared that such encouragement would depopulate the mother country and be injurious to its industrial interests. For the same reason an application for a land grant presented by petitioners proposing to establish a Scotch settlement in North Carolina was rejected.[3]

An earlier instance of the same British policy occurred when a Georgia act of March 6, 1766, was disallowed on August 26, 1767. That "Act for encouraging Settlers to come into this Prov-

[1] *Documents Relative to the Colonial History of the State of New-York,* VIII, 402. See also *ibid.,* 564.
[2] Cora Stuart, "Naturalization in the English Colonies of America," *Annual Report of the American Historical Association for the Year 1893,* 323; A. H. Carpenter, "Naturalization in England and the American Colonies," *American Historical Review,* Vol. IX, No. 2 (January, 1904), 294, 300.
[3] *The Colonial Records of North Carolina,* IX, 284, 303-304.

ince" provided that "when any number of families, being protestants, not less than forty, each family to consist at least of one man above the age of sixteen years, and one woman" arrived and proved their good character, "a township shall be immediately allotted and laid out in some convenient spot for their residence," at the public charge. A ten-year exemption from provincial taxes was also accorded to the settlers.[4]

Virginia was particularly alarmed when the terms upon which land could be obtained by grant from the crown were made less advantageous to the purchaser. An order of the King on April 7, 1773, suspended the issuance of land patents until his further pleasure was signified. Governor Martin of North Carolina issued a proclamation in accordance with that order on June 28, 1773, although he feared that because of the availability of proprietary lands the intended policy of discouraging emigration from the king's European dominions would not operate effectively in North Carolina, but would merely curtail drastically the governor's income from patent fees. Then on February 3, 1774, royal instructions were issued to the governors which required that all vacant lands be disposed of at public sale to the highest bidder, reserving to the crown an annual quit rent of one halfpenny sterling per acre, as well as all mines of gold, silver, or precious stones.[5] A proclamation pursuant to these instructions was made in Virginia by Governor Dunmore on March 21, 1775.

This was regarded as an innovation departing from the established usage of granting lands.[6] At the second Virginia Convention, the following resolution was adopted on March 27, 1775:

> *Resolved,* that a committee be appointed to inquire whether his Majesty may, of right, advance the terms of granting lands in this colony, and make report thereof to the next General Assem-

[4] *Acts of the Privy Council*, V, 112–13; *Acts Passed by the General Assembly of Georgia* [at October 24, 1765, session], 7–9.

[5] *The Colonial Records of North Carolina*, IX, 632, 667–68, 818; *Documents Relative to the Colonial History of the State of New-York*, VIII, 357–58, 410–13.

[6] Force, *American Archives*, (4th series), II, 174. Regarding the mode of acquiring lands in Virginia, see Jefferson, *Works*, IV, 45–47.

bly, or Convention; and that, in the meantime, it be recommended to all persons whatever to forbear purchasing or accepting grants of lands on the conditions before mentioned; and that Patrick Henry, Richard Bland, Thomas Jefferson, Robert Carter Nicholas, and Edmund Pendleton, Esquires, be appointed to the said committee.[7]

Jefferson had previously in his *Summary View* complained of the increasingly onerous terms imposed by the crown, "by which means the acquisition of lands being rendered difficult, the population of our country is likely to be checked."[8]

Richard Bland had written a treatise on a similar theme when Lieutenant Governor Dinwiddie in 1753 demanded a pistole fee for sealing patents for land, without any law authorizing such an exaction. "Virginians had for many years acquired new land by means of a warrant of survey, without a patent or expense. In this way they escaped the payment of any fee for a formal grant, and could enjoy the use of the land without paying a quit rent to the government." Dinwiddie refused to grant patents without payment of quit rent and the pistole fee. The Burgesses protested, and sent Peyton Randolph to London to present their case. The matter was heard by the Privy Council, where Lord Mansfield argued against them. The Council recommended a compromise, with no fee to be charged for land under one hundred acres or west of the mountains or where the survey was filed before April 22, 1752. Dinwiddie was required to reinstate Randolph as attorney general, George Wythe having held that office during Randolph's absence in England.[9]

During this dispute, "The king was at one time compared to a private land-holder, who might modify his terms with the mercenary dexterity of a huckster."[10] The House of Burgesses,

[7] *Proceedings of the Convention of Delegates*, 18–19. At the next convention a similar committee was chosen on July 18, 1775, to which Jefferson was added when he took his seat on August 9, 1775. Jefferson, *Works*, II, 98. See Jefferson, *Papers*, I, 162.

[8] Page 21.

[9] Richard Bland, *A Fragment on the Pistole Fee*, 7, 8, 10–14, 18. The address of the Burgesses was rejected on June 21, 1754. *Acts of the Privy Council*, IV, 232–35.

[10] Edmund Randolph, quoted in Moncure D. Conway, *Omitted Chapters of*

on the other hand, insisted that the governor and council could not alter the terms upon which grants were to be made, and "That whoever shall hereafter pay a Pistole, as a Fee to the Governor, for the Use of the Seal to Patents for Lands, shall be deemed a Betrayer of the Rights and Privileges of the People."[11]

HE *has obstructed the Administration of Justice, by refusing his Assent to Laws for establishing Judiciary Powers.*

This passage reads in the Rough Draft:
He has suffered the administration of justice totally to cease in some of these colonies, refusing his assent to laws for establishing judiciary powers.

The committee changed "colonies" to "states." Congress then amended the text to the form in which it now stands.

This charge refers to the situation existing in North Carolina, where as a result of controversy between governor and assembly the laws establishing courts of justice were allowed to expire, without the enactment of new legislation, and North Carolina was without courts for a considerable period of time.

This dispute was of long standing. On April 8, 1754, the government in England, upon reviewing the revised laws of North Carolina, disallowed eighteen acts,[1] including one passed in 1746 for establishing courts of justice and regulating their proceedings. Among other objections, the Lords of Trade had asserted that the erection of courts of justice was an act of sovereignty belonging to the king alone. On January 14, 1755, Governor Arthur Dobbs gave his assent to acts for the establishment of supreme courts of justice and county courts in the province.[2] These acts were disallowed by the King on April 14, 1759, upon the

---

History Disclosed in the Life and Papers of Edmund Randolph, 9. See also Lind, *An Answer to the Declaration,* 43.

[11] *Journals of the House of Burgesses of Virginia, 1752–1755,* 155 (resolution of December 4, 1753). See also, for the course of this dispute, *ibid., xviii,* 132, 136, 141, 143–44, 154–56, 166–69.

[1] *The Colonial Records of North Carolina,* V, 108, 116–18.
[2] *Ibid.,* 279.

ground that the county courts, composed of "unlettered persons," were given too great a jurisdiction (over cases up to £40); and that the act delegated to the associate judges of the supreme courts a power to hold court in the absence of the chief justice, which could only be delegated by the crown.[3] The Governor, lest there "be a stagnation of Justice," did not announce the repeal of the court laws until the assembly met. A court bill was then debated, but was rejected by the Council when the House refused to impose a new tax to pay judicial salaries, and the Governor dissolved the assembly on January 9, 1760.[4] At a subsequent session, a superior court bill substantially identical with that which had been repealed in England was rejected by the Governor, but when re-enacted with a clause making it temporary for two years until the King's pleasure could be known, the Governor reluctantly gave his assent on May 27, 1760. This legislation was disallowed by the King on December 14, 1761, and Governor Dobbs was reprimanded severely for having approved its enactment. He announced these developments to the assembly on November 3, 1762.[5] On December 11, 1762, new court bills were enacted after some disagreement between the Council and the House.[6]

This legislation, which was continued in force from time to time, seemed satisfactory to the government in England, although the Governor was instructed to ask that the assembly make provision for the judicial establishment and salaries upon a permanent basis.[7] Later, however, exception was taken to a provision in the acts of January 15, 1768, carried forward from those of 1762, authorizing the attachment of property belonging to nonresidents who had never been in the colony. Strife over this attachment provision led to the situation described in the Declaration of Independence, as the result of which there were no courts in North Carolina for a considerable period of time.

[3] *Ibid.*, VI, 13–15, 28–29, 69–72.

[4] *Ibid.*, 56, 134, 172–80, 331.

[5] *Ibid.*, 401, 409, 419, 420–21, 425, 628, 839.

[6] *Ibid.*, 862–68, 872, 890, 970.

[7] *Ibid.*, 1049, 1054; VII, 551.

The government in England regarded the attachment provision as being contrary to English law,[8] but the assembly unflinchingly maintained that such a provision was necessary for the commerce of the province, and was permitted in neighboring colonies.[9] A bill including the attachment provision, covering both superior and inferior courts, but with a suspending clause, was passed and approved by the Governor on March 6, 1773.[10]

The court laws of 1768 expired by their own terms when the assembly was dissolved by the Governor on March 9, 1773. Since the act of March 6, 1773, was unacceptable to the King and never went into effect, North Carolina was without courts of justice established by law.[11] In the absence of statutory authority, Governor Martin proceeded to hold criminal courts of oyer and terminer under royal prerogative. His right to do so was denied by the House at the next session of assembly. The English government upheld his power to establish courts, but recommended that no civil courts be so established unless necessary.[12]

When the next assembly met on December 4, 1773, the contest continued. On March 24, 1774, after the colony had been without any court laws at all for over a year, the Governor assented with displeasure to bills for establishing inferior courts and courts of oyer and terminer. After that date he never permitted the assembly to sit again, except for a few days in the spring of 1775.[13] North Carolina thus remained without superior courts until they were established by authority of the people of the state after the Revolution had begun and the royal government had been discarded.

8 *Ibid.*, VIII, 265; IX, 681, 988, 997–99, 1252. Under English law, attachment was available only against absconding debtors.

9 *Ibid.*, IX, 558–59, 730–32, 795–98, 820, 965, 1174–75. It was sometimes thought that the tenacity with which the assembly contended for the attachment provision was due to the fact that the pretty widow of Governor Dobbs had been left a legacy of £2,000 charged upon an estate given to a younger son in Ireland who had never been in North Carolina and who evinced no disposition to make payment. *Ibid.*, IX, *xxii*, 995–96, 1210.

10 *Ibid.*, 435–38, 442, 444, 446, 619–20. At the same time he disapproved the separate inferior court and superior court bills which had been passed containing the attachment provision. *Ibid.*, 446, 447.

11 *Ibid.*, 599, 681.

12 *Ibid.*, 686, 743, 794–95, 816, 988–89.

13 *Ibid.*, IX, 862, 870–71, 1009–10, 1187–1205.

Besides the controversy over the North Carolina court laws, the rejection by the crown of a South Carolina law of April 12, 1768, may have been regarded by the framers of the Declaration of Independence as an instance of obstructing the administration of justice by refusing assent to laws for establishing judiciary powers. Inhabitants of the back country in South Carolina complained of having to travel two hundred miles to Charleston to attend court, claiming that this deprived them of their constitutional right to trial by a jury of the vicinage. In response to the clamor of the people for courts more conveniently located, the act of April 12, 1768, was passed, after a bargain had first been made to compensate the English dramatist Richard Cumberland for the loss of his profits as absentee holder of the office of provost marshal, which would be abolished by the establishment of new courts. The King on October 7, 1768, disallowed this law, because the provision it made for salaries of the judges was contingent upon their appointment during good behavior instead of during the king's pleasure. So insistent was the demand for courts that the assembly yielded its claim to tenure during good behavior and a new act of July 29, 1769, was passed, complying with the requirements imposed by the King.[14]

In Pennsylvania, also, the disallowance of court laws had on several occasions caused the normal administration of justice "totally to cease." This occurred when an order in council of February 7, 1706, disallowed 52 out of 105 Pennsylvania laws reviewed in England, including the act of October 28, 1701, for establishing courts of judicature. On that occasion Lieutenant Governor John Evans noted that "thereupon an entire failure in the administration of justice in this province has ensued." Accordingly, by an ordinance of February 22, 1707, issued by virtue of powers granted to the Proprietor of Pennsylvania under the charter of Charles II, he created courts to replace those abolished by repeal of the statute. Again a few years later when the act of February 28, 1711, was repealed by an order in council on February

[14] Edward McCrady, *The History of South Carolina under the Royal Government*, 633-42; William R. Smith, *South Carolina as a Royal Province*, 134-38; *Acts of the General Assembly of South Carolina. Passed the 12th of April, 1768*, 3-15; *Acts of the Privy Council*, V, 166-71.

20, 1714, Lieutenant Governor Charles Gookin on July 20, 1714, issued a similar ordinance setting up a system of courts to maintain the administration of justice in the province.[15]

Moreover, the administration of justice was suddenly brought to a standstill in Virginia when it was learned on April 8, 1752, that the King had disallowed ten laws, including those for the establishment of the General Court and several county courts. The very next day the House of Burgesses and the council passed a law declaring valid the proceedings of the General Court during the period between the enactment and the disallowance of the act rejected by the crown. Lieutenant Governor Dinwiddie obligingly gave his assent on the same day. Soon afterward a similar bill was passed with respect to the local courts in six counties, including Albemarle and Augusta,[16] where Jefferson later practiced law.

HE *has made Judges dependent on his Will alone, for the Tenure of their Offices, and the Amount and Payment of their Salaries.*

This passage reads in the Rough Draft:
He has made our judges dependent on his will alone, for the tenure of their offices, and amount of their salaries.

Congress deleted "our," and Franklin in the committee changed the concluding words to read "the Amount and Payment of their Salaries."

This grievance was experienced in Pennsylvania, New York, New Jersey, North Carolina, South Carolina, and Massachusetts. Although the tenure of judges during good behavior had been guaranteed in England since the Act of Settlement in 1701,[1] the

[15] *The Statutes at Large of Pennsylvania*, II, 456, 501; 543, 556. For other court laws disallowed, see *ibid.*, III, 440; IV, 421; V, 655.

[16] *Journals of the House of Burgesses of Virginia 1752–1755*, *xv*, 78, 81, 82, 89–97.

[1] Act of June 12, 1701, 12 and 13 Wm. III, c. 2, sec. 3. George B. Adams and H. M. Stephens, *Select Documents of English Constitutional History*, 479. Section 4 of the same act contained another provision which the Colonists cited in the controversy over their constitutional rights: "the laws of England are the birthright of the people thereof."

English government in 1761 insisted that the tenure of Colonial judges should be at the king's pleasure. In that year the New York judges refused to act unless their commissions under the new king were for tenure during good behavior, as their former commissions had read, because of Governor Clinton's laxity. The New York legislature also passed a bill providing for such tenure, but Lieutenant Governor Cadwallader Colden refused to approve it and brought the subject to the attention of the British government. Whereupon instructions were sent to the Colonial governors on December 2, 1761, forbidding upon pain of removal from office their giving assent to any act regulating the tenure of judges in any manner whatever. It was ordered that all commissions should be during the king's pleasure only.

The British government claimed that the rule appropriate in England was not suitable to the situation of the Colonies. In the mother country the independence of the judges was assured not only by their tenure but by fixed salaries, which were not provided in the Colonies. Moreover, unless judges were removable at the king's pleasure, an unfit person, who might have obtained office because of the scarcity of properly qualified lawyers in the Colonies, could not be displaced even though a more fit person might afterwards be found.[2]

In New Jersey the question of tenure led to a bitter dispute which resulted in the removal of Governor Josiah Hardy. Chief Justice Robert Hunter Morris, who held a commission dated March 17, 1738, during good behavior, resigned. His resignation was never formally accepted, but a successor was appointed and served until his death. Thereupon Morris, desiring to resume his office, did so. His colleagues on the New Jersey court on March 18, 1760, recognized his right to serve, and according-

[2] *Documents Relative to the Colonial History of the State of New-York,* VII, 468–79. See also *ibid.,* 489, 503–506, 796; and Labaree, *Royal Instructions,* I, 367–68; *Documents Relating to the Colonial History of the State of New Jersey,* IX, 321–30; Russell, *Review of American Colonial Legislation,* 190; Evarts B. Greene, *The Provincial Governor,* 135–36; *Acts of the Privy Council,* IV, 551, 807. The first Colonial act attempting to establish tenure during good behavior was passed in Jamaica in 1751, and was disallowed on February 28, 1754. *Ibid.,* IV, 216–17. A New York law of December 31, 1761, granting salaries to the judges upon condition that they held commissions during good behavior, was disallowed on August 12, 1762.

ly refused to administer the oath of office to Nathaniel Jones, who had been appointed by the crown to fill the vacancy. The attorney general of England gave an opinion on January 18, 1763, adverse to Morris's claim. Apparently the British government believed that Governor Hardy was responsible for the violation of instructions with respect to tenure during pleasure in the case of Morris. By letter of September 11, 1762, Hardy was notified of his removal as governor. As a matter of fact, he had two months previously reported to the government in England that their commissions during good behavior had been relinquished by the New Jersey judges.[3]

Tenure during good behavior was prescribed by a Pennsylvania act passed on September 29, 1759, supplementing the prior act of May 22, 1722, for establishing courts of judicature. The King in council on September 2, 1760, disallowed the audacious innovation.[4] A North Carolina court law of May 27, 1760, containing the same provision, was disallowed on December 14, 1761, and Governor Arthur Dobbs was reprimanded for having assented to it.[5] A South Carolina act of April 12, 1768, subject to the same infirmity, was disallowed on October 7, 1768.[6]

Other types of laws relating to the organization of courts and the administration of justice also were often regarded by the crown as infringements upon the royal prerogative.[7]

In Massachusetts one of the bones of contention in the chronic controversy between Governor Hutchinson and the legislature was the matter of official salaries. The assembly contended that its own grants should constitute the sole support of the governor and judges, and that they should not be dependent upon the crown for their subsistence.

[3] *Documents Relating to the Colonial History of the State of New Jersey,* IX, 176, 206–209, 214–18, 270–73, 324, 361–62, 364–65, 374, 426–27.

[4] *Acts of the Privy Council,* IV, 808; *The Statutes at Large of Pennsylvania,* V, 463, 722–24. See also *ibid.,* VI, 567–71.

[5] *The Colonial Records of North Carolina,* VI, 425, 588, 592, 628, 839; *Acts of the Privy Council,* IV, 502.

[6] *Acts of the Privy Council,* V, 169. See page 111 above.

[7] Russell, *Review of American Colonial Legislation,* 165–67; George A. Washburne, *Imperial Control of the Administration of Justice,* 180–81; *Acts of the Privy Council,* II, 841, 847; IV, 59, 139; V, 285, 320.

DUNLAP BROADSIDE

On May 30, 1771, the House inquired of Governor Hutchinson if he had assented to a bill providing for his salary, or whether he was receiving support from another source. In response to a similar inquiry on June 6, 1772, the Governor answered, a week later, that the crown had made provision for him, in accordance with an act of Parliament. On July 10, 1772, the House adopted resolutions declaring this to be a grievance.[8] In response to a complaint by Hutchinson regarding the dilapidated state of his official residence, the House on July 14, 1772, declared their willingness to provide an elegant mansion for a governor supported by themselves, but not for a royal hireling.[9]

On October 28, 1772, a Boston town meeting expressed alarm at a report that the judges were receiving stipends from the crown, and two days later urged that the assembly be permitted to meet. Governor Hutchinson considered these actions by the town of Boston as outside the province of a town meeting and as invasions of the royal prerogative. On February 3, 1773, the House desired to be informed why the Governor had not assented to grants for the salaries of the judges. Hutchinson replied that he did not wish to duplicate the sums they received from the crown. The House demanded assurance that the judges refused to accept support from the crown. Upon the Governor's reply that he could not inform the assembly of such refusal, a resolution was adopted on March 3, 1773, declaring that it was unconstitutional for the judges to be independent of the people and dependent on the crown; and that any judge accepting support from the crown would show himself to be an enemy of the constitution.[10]

HE *has erected a Multitude of new Offices, and sent hither Swarms of Officers to harrass our People, and eat out their Substance.*

Congress deleted from the Rough Draft the words "by a self-assumed power" after "new Offices."

[8] *Massachusetts State Papers*, 298, 324–30.
[9] *Ibid.*, 330–31.
[10] *Ibid.*, 365–67, 396–98; Wells, *Life and Public Services of Samuel Adams*, , 491–96.

The "new Offices" and "Swarms of Officers" here referred to are the commissioners of customs and additional courts of admiralty.[1]

The British government in 1764, during Grenville's administration, proposed to enforce the trade laws and prevent smuggling.[2] Provision was made in the Sugar Act that offenses against the revenue might be tried by courts of admiralty and vice-admiralty: "all the forfeitures and penalties inflicted by this or any other act or acts of parliament relating to the trade and revenues of the said British colonies or plantations in America, which shall be incurred there, shall and may be prosecuted, sued for, and recovered in any court of record, or in any court of admiralty, in the said colonies or plantations where such offence shall be committed, or in any court of vice admiralty which may or shall be appointed over all America (which court of admiralty or vice admiralty are hereby respectively authorized and required to proceed, hear, and determine the same) at the election of the informer or prosecutor."[3] The first such court was opened in Halifax in 1764. A later act provided that after September 1, 1768, such proceedings might be had "in any court of vice-admiralty appointed, or to be appointed, and which shall have jurisdiction within the colony, plantation, or place, where the cause of such prosecution or suit shall have arisen."[4] The act recited that for such cases to be tried "in one court only of vice-admiralty over all America, may, in many cases, by reason of the distance of the places where the cause of such suits and prosecutions shall arise from the place where such court is or shall be established, be attended with great inconvenience."

The new resident commissioners of customs were authorized by an act passed in 1766 to exercise the same powers as the com-

[1] Lind, *An Answer to the Declaration*, 48–50; Hutchinson, *Strictures*, 19. According to Hutchinson, the "swarms" of new officers would number between thirty and forty, including fifteen or twenty clerks. Only "illicit traders" would be injured by the activities of these officers, and that by being "better watched than they had ever been before."

[2] William Knox, *The Controversy between Great Britain and her Colonies Reviewed*, 44.

[3] 4 Geo. III, c. 15, sec. 41.

[4] 8 Geo. III, c. 22. For the order of July 6, 1768, establishing four such courts, see *Acts of the Privy Council*, V, 151–53.

missioners of the customs had theretofore possessed in England.[5] They were paid by fees. Their appointment was considered by the home government as a measure of convenience to the colonists, whose affairs would otherwise have been subject to delays due to the necessity of obtaining instructions from the more distant commissioners in England.

A protest against the acts of 4 Geo. III, c. 15 and 7 Geo. III, c. 41 was made in the resolutions of the Continental Congress in 1774.[6] Similarly the Massachusetts House had remonstrated against this legislation on October 23, 1765, June 29, 1769, and July 5, 1771.[7]

HE *has kept among us, in Times of Peace, Standing Armies, without the consent of our Legislatures.*

In the Rough Draft this passage reads:
He has kept among us in times of peace standing armies & ships of war.

The committee added "without our consent," later making the addition read "without the consent of our Legislatures." Congress deleted the reference to "ships of war."

It was a fundamental principle of English liberty that a standing army could not be kept up in time of peace without the consent of Parliament. The Bill of Rights of December 16, 1689, declared "That the raising or keeping a standing army within the kingdom in time of peace unless it be with consent of parliament is against law." In the same instrument is a recital that "the late King James the Second . . . did endeavour to subvert . . . the laws and liberties of this kingdom . . . By raising and keeping a standing army within the kingdom in time of peace, without consent of parliament, and quartering of soldiers contrary to law."[1]

On the colonists' assumption that their local legislatures held, with respect to them, the same position as Parliament in England,

[5] 7 Geo. III, c. 41.
[6] *Journals*, I, 71.
[7] *Massachusetts State Papers*, 47, 179, 307.
[1] 1 Wm. and Mary, 2 sess., c. 2, in George B. Adams and H. M. Stephens, *Select Documents of English Constitutional History*, 463–64.

it is obvious that the grievance here complained of was a serious one. Indeed, as Jefferson stated in his *Summary View*, if the king possessed "such a right as this, it might swallow up all our other rights whenever he should think proper."[2]

To the English, of course, on the other hand, it seemed axiomatic that troops could be stationed wherever it was thought advisable.[3]

After the peace of 1763 terminating the Seven Years' War with France, the troops were not withdrawn. The Quartering Act of April, 1765, made the Colonies liable for their support.[4] Several companies of royal artillery were stationed at Boston after the Stamp Act riots of 1766. The assembly on February 4, 1767, remonstrated with the Governor against their being quartered at the expense of the province without an appropriation by the assembly.[5] In 1768, in anticipation of enforcement of the Townshend Act,[6] more troops were sent to Boston, New York, and other points. After the Boston Massacre of March 5, 1770, the troops took over the provincial garrison at Castle William. This led to further controversy between the Governor and the assembly in Massachusetts.[7]

HE *has affected to render the Military independent of and superior to the Civil Power.*

This refers to the appointment of General Gage as governor of Massachusetts in 1774 while he was commander in chief of the British troops in America.[1]

In Jefferson's draft of a declaration on taking up arms, he refers to the proclamation of June 12, 1775, in which Gage declares "the good people of these colonies" to be "rebels and traitors," and proceeds to "supersede by his own authority the exercise of

---

[2] Page 21.

[3] Lind, *An Answer to the Declaration*, 51–52.

[4] 5 Geo. III, c. 33.

[5] *Massachusetts State Papers*, 105–108.

[6] See page 5 above and page 131 below.

[7] *Ibid.*, 256, 258–73, 387–89, 293; Thomas Hutchinson, *Diary*, I, 29–30.

[1] Soon after taking office, Gage abruptly dissolved the assembly. *Massachusetts State Papers*, 416.

the common law" of Massachusetts "and to proclaim and order instead thereof the use and exercise of the law martial."[2]

On April 15, 1775, the Colonial governors had been notified by the English government that the "orders of the Commander in Chief of his Majesty's forces in North America, and under him of the Major Generals and Brigadier Generals shall be supreme in all cases relative to the operations of the said troops, and be obeyed accordingly."[3] Some years earlier a "disagreeable dispute" between General Gage and Governor Moore of New York had broken out as a result of the military officer's claim to precedence on all occasions.[4]

It is interesting to note that while Jefferson in the Declaration condemns the union of civil and military powers in the same official, he withdrew as governor of Virginia during the Revolution in favor of a soldier: "From a belief that under the pressure of the invasion under which we were then laboring the public would have more confidence in a Military chief, and that the Military commander, being invested with the civil power also, both might be wielded with more energy promptitude and effect for the defence of the state, I resigned the administration at the end of my 2d. year, and General Nelson was appointed to succeed me."[5] John Quincy Adams regarded that action on Jefferson's part as "anti-republican."[6]

OBNOXIOUS ACTS OF PRETENDED LEGISLATION

HE *has combined with others to subject us to a Jurisdiction foreign to our Constitution, and unacknowledged by our Laws; giving his Assent to their Acts of pretended Legislation:*

The committee changed "pretended acts of legislation" to "Acts of pretended Legislation."

[2] *Journals*, II, 137. For the text of Gage's proclamation, see Force, *American Archives* (4th series), II, 968–70. See also Jefferson, *Summary View*, 21–22.

[3] *Documents Relative to the Colonial History of the State of New-York*, VIII, 569.

[4] *Ibid.*, 16, 73, 97–98. For comment in Parliament on the relationship between civil and military officers, see *Parliamentary History*, XVI, 979–1001.

[5] Jefferson, *Works*, I, 79.

[6] John Quincy Adams, *Memoirs*, VIII, 294–96.

At this point in the Declaration, the acts of Parliament are enumerated which the Americans regarded as an unconstitutional exercise of authority.[1] The King is condemned for having "combined with others" to enact these offensive statutes; that is to say, for assenting to legislation and failing to exercise his veto power. An earlier charge in the Declaration denounced his having exercised the power of disallowance in the case of American laws "the most wholesome and necessary for the public Good."[2]

The unidentified "others" with whom the King is charged with combining were, obviously, the Lords and Commons in Parliament. As a former royal governor of Massachusetts said, "This is a strange way of defining the part which the Kings of England take in conjunction with the Lords and Commons in passing Acts of Parliament."[3] Of course, it is essential to the enactment of an English statute that the formula of royal assent be pronounced: "*Le roy le veult.*"[4]

The charge here made against the King and his co-conspirators in Parliament brings to a focus the major issue of the Revolution: What was the scope of Parliament's constitutional authority to legislate for America? The Declaration asserts squarely that, with respect to certain specified instances at least, Parliament possessed no legislative power whatever over the Colonies.

The same conclusion had been proclaimed even more plainly in Jefferson's *Summary View,* where he asserted in 1774 that "the British Parliament has no right to exercise authority over us," it being "a body of men, foreign to our constitutions, and unacknowledged by our laws."[5]

Implicit in the phrase "our Constitution" is Jefferson's theory of the relationship between the Colonies and the home government. The Declaration does not speak of "the British Constitution" or even of "the Constitution of the Empire," but of "*our*"

[1] An eminent writer regards this passage in the Declaration as a precursor of the doctrine of judicial review. For it treats as unconstitutional Parliament's "Acts of pretended Legislation." McLaughlin, *The Foundations of American Constitutionalism,* 120, 155.

[2] See page 87 above.

[3] Lind, *An Answer to the Declaration,* 56; Hutchinson, *Strictures,* 20.

[4] Josef Redlich, *The Procedure of the House of Commons,* III, 109; *Annual Report of the American Bar Association* (1947), LXXII, 328.

[5] Pages 11, 16.

Constitution. Only a constitution based upon the consent of Americans could create authority to make law for and govern America. The power of the king, or of Parliament, was lawful only to the extent that such power can be shown to have been delegated to them by the people of the Colonies.

It is Jefferson's position, especially as developed in his *Summary View*, that such a delegation did take place. He interprets the history of the Colonies as showing that each colony did grant certain powers to the English government. Thereby, and to that extent, those rulers residing abroad became a part of the American "machine of government."

The colonists immediately upon their arrival in America, according to this theory, were in a "state of nature." To establish political society, they entered, by their voluntary consent, into a "social compact." The government which they thus established resembled, to the degree that local conditions permitted, the government they had enjoyed in England. They preserved the traditional rights and liberties of Englishmen. They adopted as their law the common law of England, so far as it was applicable to circumstances in their new country. They chose the king of England as their chief executive.

Upon the completion of this process in every colony, the colonies were perfectly independent of each other. Each one was a separate and distinct society, but was united with the others, and with "our British brethren," through the crown. The same person happened to be chief executive of these otherwise unconnected states. As Jefferson wrote in a passage of the Declaration which Congress omitted, "we had adopted one common king, thereby laying a foundation for perpetual league and amity with them," but "submission to their parliament was no part of our constitution." The British legislature would have no greater authority over New York, for example, than would the Pennsylvania or Virginia legislature. Whatever powers the British Parliament had exercised were founded on the "acquiescence" or common consent of the Colonies.

This argument was advanced in Congress during the debates in June, 1776, regarding the advisability of a declaration of independence. Those favoring such a step contended:

That as to the people or parliament of England, we had always been independent of them, their restraints on our trade deriving efficacy from our acquiescence only & not from any rights they possessed of imposing them, & that so far our connection had been federal only & was now dissolved by the commencement of hostilities:

That as to the king, we had been bound to him by allegiance, but that this bond was now dissolved by his assent to the late act of parliament, by which he declares us out of his protection,[6] and by his levying war on us, a fact which had long ago proved us out of his protection; . . . that allegiance & protection are reciprocal, the one ceasing when the other is withdrawn:

That James the IId. never declared the people of England out of his protection yet his actions proved it & the parliament declared it.[7]

Thus the Declaration of Independence was intended to proclaim on behalf of the Colonies, as Parliament had done in the case of James II, that the monarch chosen by them to be their ruler had been ousted from "the kingly office" by reason of his violation of the compact betwixt king and people. Upon severance of this connection, there would be no ties with England remaining, for no allegiance was owed to Parliament. The second Continental Congress, replying on December 6, 1775, to the King's proclamation of August 23, 1775, had explicitly enunciated: "We are accused of 'forgetting the allegiance we owe to the power that has protected and sustained us.' What allegiance is it that we forget? Allegiance to Parliament? We never owed—we never owned it. Allegiance to the King? Our words have ever avowed it,—our conduct has ever been consistent with it. We condemn . . . and oppose the claim and exercise of unconstitutional powers, to which neither the crown nor Parliament were ever entitled."[8]

[6] 16 Geo. III, c. 5. See page 12 above and page 130 below.

[7] Jefferson, *Works*, I, 22, 24–25 (spelling modernized). See also *ibid.*, II, 112–13; and Jefferson, *Writings*, XVII, 411–12.

[8] *Journals*, III, 410.

The traditional pattern of constitutional liberty, which was cherished both in England and in the Colonies, emphasized the part played by the representatives of the people in the conduct of public business, and sought to strengthen and preserve the rights and privileges that had been won for them in the course of an eventful struggle against the arbitrary power of the king. This historic heritage was treasured equally by English and American statesmen. The difficulty which led to misunderstanding was that in England the body which represented the people and protected them against tyrannical exercise of power by the crown was Parliament, whereas in America the body which represented the people was each colony's local assembly. To Americans, the British legislature was as remote and unfriendly as the king. It was an alien body, "foreign to our Constitution," though performing for "our British brethren" the functions appertaining to that branch of government which gave expression to the popular will.

To Englishmen, it seemed not "liberal" but a reversion to Stuart tyranny for the crown to act independently of Parliament in exercising political power. Yet Jefferson in the Declaration and in his *Summary View* was urging that the king should veto acts of the British legislature because they interfered with measures deemed expedient by American legislatures. To the "deep question" whether the king could accept a revenue granted by a colony, without regard to the wishes of the British Parliament, Benjamin Franklin gave an affirmative answer; but to English ears this must have seemed like a dangerous extension of the powers of the crown. It was not then recognized throughout the British Empire that a single "common king," in Jefferson's phrase, could serve as a part of the governmental machinery of a multitude of self-governing commonwealths.

In England, Parliament represented the people. It was the force in English polity making for self-government. But in America this British legislature did not and could not represent the people. The people of the Colonies had other parliaments of their own. By these they were represented. Through these, their own local assemblies, they exercised the valued privileges that after long-continued contest between crown and people had been confirmed as constitutional rights which were the birthright of every British subject. Across the seas from London the true spirit of reverence for parliamentary institutions as an instrument of popular government had been transplanted and was bearing fruit in new soil. Not because a legislative body happens to sit in the time-honored precincts of Westminster Hall, but because it genuinely expresses the will of the people over whom it rules, is it vested with rightful jurisdiction and authority under the principles of political wisdom embodied in "our Constitution."

FOR *quartering large Bodies of Armed Troops among us:*

The corrected Journal omits the word "Armed." This is an error in copying rather than a correction.

First listed among the offensive English acts of legislation for America are those providing for the quartering of troops in the Colonies.[1] It was adding injury to insult to require the Americans to pay for the maintenance of an army kept among them without the consent of their own legislatures.

The Quartering Act of June 2, 1774 (14 Geo. III, c. 54) was one of the five "Intolerable Acts" which led to the meeting of the first Continental Congress.[2] This act was meant to make the Colonies responsible for quarters at the spot where troops were employed, even if barracks were available in the vicinity. The new statute was designed to obviate the argument made in 1768 that until the barracks at Castle William, three miles out from Boston, were filled, Massachusetts could not be required to furnish quarters in town, even when the troops were sent to America because of commotion in that town.[3]

After a preamble reciting:

Whereas doubts have been entertained, whether troops can be quartered otherwise than in barracks, in case barracks have been

[1] Lind, *An Answer to the Declaration*, 59.

[2] See page 7 above. For debate in Parliament on this act, see Force, *American Archives* (4th series), I, 166–70.

[3] Alexander Elmsly to Samuel Johnston, May 17, 1774, *Colonial Records of North Carolina*, IX, 1001; Wells, *Life and Public Services of Samuel Adams*, I, 220.

provided sufficient for the quartering of all the officers and soldiers within any town, township, city, district, or place, within his Majesty's dominions in North America: And whereas it may frequently happen, from the situation of such barracks, that, if troops should be quartered therein, they would not be stationed where their presence may be necessary and required

the act of 1774 made it lawful in such cases:

to cause any officers or soldiers in his Majesty's service to be quartered and billetted in such manner as is now directed by law, where no barracks are provided by the colonies.

It was further enacted that if any officers or soldiers remained without quarters twenty-four hours after demand therefor, the governor of the province was empowered:

to order and direct such and so many uninhabited houses, outhouses, barns, or other buildings, as he shall think necessary to be taken . . . and to put and quarter such officers and soldiers therein, for such time as he shall think proper.

The colonists' contentions with respect to earlier quartering acts[4] which caused controversy in America were justified by the language of the statutes. While the Mutiny Act applicable in England (5 Geo. III, c. 7) prohibited quartering of troops in private houses, the act extending this legislation to America (5 Geo. III, c. 33) permitted private houses to be taken under certain circumstances. The civil officers authorized to provide quarters in the Colonies were directed first "to quarter and billet the officers and soldiers, in his Majesty's service, in the barracks provided by the colonies; and *if there shall not be sufficient room in the said barracks for the officers and soldiers, then and in such case only*, to quarter and billet the residue of such officers and soldiers, for whom there shall not be room in such barracks, in inns, livery-stables," and similar "publick houses." If these did

[4] 5 Geo. III, c. 7; 5 Geo. III, c. 33; 6 Geo. III, c. 8; 6 Geo. III, c. 18; 7 Geo. III, c. 55.

not suffice, the appropriate officials were required to utilize "such and so many uninhabited houses, outhouses, barns, or other buildings, as shall be necessary" for quartering the "residue" which could not be accommodated "in such barracks and publick houses as aforesaid."

Section VII of the act provided that officers and soldiers in quarters should be "furnished and supplied there . . . with fire, candles, vinegar, and salt, bedding, utensils for dressing their victuals, and small beer or cyder, not exceeding five pints, or half a pint of rum mixed with a quart of water, to each man, without paying any thing for the same." Section VIII of the act, in order to reimburse the persons providing quarters and necessaries for the troops, commanded "*That the respective provinces shall pay unto such person or persons, all such sum or sums of money* so by them paid, laid out, or expended, for the taking, hiring, and fitting up, such uninhabited houses, out-houses, barns, or other buildings, and for furnishing the officers and soldiers therein, and in the barracks, with fire, candles, vinegar, and salt, bedding, utensils for dressing victuals, and small beer, cyder, or rum, as aforesaid; *and such sum or sums are hereby required to be raised, in such manner as the publick charges for the provinces respectively are raised.*"[5]

Strong resentment was aroused in America when Parliament suspended the legislature of New York because its act of July 6, 1766,[6] did not comply fully with the requirements of the quartering acts. The New York act failed to provide for salt, vinegar, and liquor, which were then felt to be ruinously expensive luxuries. On account of this omission Parliament thundered that "the house of representatives of his Majesty's province of *New York* in *America* have, in direct disobedience of the authority of the *British* legislature, refused to make provision for supplying the necessaries and in the manner required by the said act; and an act of assembly hath been passed, within the said province, for

[5] Italics supplied. The provinces were similarly required by Section XX of the act to pay for carriages hired for transporting troops. Later acts cited in note 4 above continued in force the provisions already described.

[6] *Colonial Laws of New York*, IV, 901–903. This act was repealed by the King on April 13, 1767. A New Jersey act of June 24, 1767, was disallowed on August 12, 1768, for the same reason. *Acts of the Privy Council*, V, 157.

furnishing the barracks in the cities of *New York* and *Albany* with firewood and candles, and other necessaries therein mentioned, for his Majesty's forces, inconsistent with the provisions, and in opposition to the directions, of the said act of parliament." The exercise of any legislative power by the New York assembly was forbidden until after provision had been made for furnishing "all such necessaries" as the quartering acts required.

The Suspending Act[7] was considered by John Dickinson in his *Farmer's Letters* to be "as injurious in its principles to the liberties of these colonies, as the Stamp Act was." Dickinson likewise condemned the provisions of the quartering acts, which the suspension act sought to enforce, as being in substance the equivalent of a tax imposed by Parliament.[8]

A reminiscence of this grievance is preserved in the Third Amendment to the Constitution of the United States. This article of the American bill of rights ordains that: "No soldier shall, in time of peace be quartered in any house, without the consent of the owner, nor in time of war, but in a manner to be prescribed by law."

For *protecting them, by a mock Trial, from Punishment for any Murders which they should commit on the Inhabitants of these States:*

The English troops were protected from punishment by the so-called "Act for the impartial administration of justice in the cases of persons questioned for any acts done by them in the execution of the law, or for the suppression of riots and tumults, in the province of the Massachuset's Bay, in New England" of May 20, 1774.[1]

That act was passed with the Boston Massacre of March 5, 1770, in mind. It provided that in prosecutions for murder or other capital offense in Massachusetts, if it appear "by informa-

---

[7] Act of June 15, 1767, 7 Geo. III, c. 59. See page 139 below.

[8] Dickinson, *Letters from a Farmer*, 7–8. The italicized language of Section VIII on page 126 above lends strong support to Dickinson's contention.

[1] 14 Geo. III, c. 39. For debate in Parliament on this act, see Force, *American Archives* (4th series), I, 111–32.

tion given on oath to the governor" that the act charged was committed by the person accused "either in the execution of his duty as a magistrate, for the suppression of riots, or in the support of the laws of revenue, or in acting in his duty as an officer of revenue, or in acting under the direction and order of any magistrate, for the suppression of riots, or for the carrying into effect the laws of revenue, or in aiding or assisting in any of the cases aforesaid," and if it also appear to the satisfaction of the governor "that an indifferent [impartial] trial cannot be had within the said province," the governor, with the advice and consent of the council, may direct that the case "be tried in some other of his Majesty's colonies, or in Great Britain." The act further empowered and required the governor to take surety for the appearance at such trial of all witnesses whose attendance is desired by the prosecutor or defendant. The governor "shall thereupon appoint a reasonable sum to be allowed for the expences of every such witness."

This act was condemned by Jefferson in his *Summary View* and by the Continental Congress in 1774.[2]

Jefferson, in his comments on this statute, seems to assume that it could apply to an American defendant:

By the act for the suppression of riots and tumults in the town of Boston, passed also in the last session of parliament, a murder committed there is, if the governor pleases, to be tried in the court of King's Bench, in the island of Great Britain, by a jury of Middlesex. The witnesses, too, on receipt of such a sum as the governor shall think it reasonable for them to expend, are to enter into recognizance to appear at the trial. This is, in other words, taxing them to the amount of their recognizance, and that amount may be whatever a governor pleases; for who does his majesty think can be prevailed on to cross the Atlantic for the sole purpose of bearing evidence to a fact? His expences are to be borne, indeed, as they shall be estimated by a governor; but who are to feed the wife and children whom he leaves behind, and who have had no other subsistence but his daily labour? Those epidemical disorders, too, so terrible in a foreign climate, is the cure of them to be estimated among the articles of expence, and their danger to be

[2] *Journals,* I, 66, 72, 87; Jefferson, *Summary View,* 15.

warded off by the almighty power of parliament? And the wretched criminal, if he happen to have offended on the American side, stripped of his privilege of trial by peers of his vicinage, removed from the place where alone full evidence could be obtained, without money, without counsel, without friends, without exculpatory proof, is tried before judges predetermined to condemn. The cowards who would suffer a countryman to be torn from the bowels of their society, in order to be thus offered a sacrifice to parliamentary tyranny, would merit that everlasting infamy now fixed on the authors of the act!

In his draft of a *Declaration on Taking up Arms* in 1775, Jefferson appears to make the same assumption that "an American colonist charged with the offenses described in that act may be transported beyond sea for trial."[3]

It seems hard to imagine, however, that there would ever be occasion for an American to be charged with having committed murder in enforcing the odious revenue laws or in suppressing the patriotic exuberance of the Sons of Liberty in Massachusetts. The act would ordinarily be invoked only in the case of English troops, such as Captain Preston and his men, who were tried for participation in the Boston Massacre.[4]

For *cutting off our Trade with all Parts of the World:*

When the Declaration here speaks of "cutting off our Trade with all Parts of the World," it doubtless refers both to the long-standing economic grievance inflicted upon the Colonies by England's mercantilist trade-regulation laws, and also to the more recent acts of 1774 and 1775 which drastically prohibited all trade with the Colonies.

The former category embraced approximately fifty acts, beginning with the notorious Navigation Act of 1660 (12 Charles II, c. 18), which gave effect to the policy of monopolizing in

[3] *Works*, II, 115.

[4] Thomas Hutchinson, *The History of . . . Massachusetts Bay*, III, 273, 327–28.

English hands all trade with America.[1] Americans regarded this monopoly as equivalent to taxation,[2] and for this reason considered imposition of taxes by Parliament to be unjust as well as unconstitutional.[3]

The latter category included the Boston Port Act of March 31, 1774,[4] and later legislation which completely shut off American trade with the rest of the world.[5] The first restraining act of March 30, 1775, applied only to Massachusetts and other northern colonies, while that of April 15, 1775, dealt with the trade of southern colonies. New York, Delaware, North Carolina, and Georgia were not affected; but they patriotically refrained from taking advantage of this exemption. Both of these acts were repealed by the prohibitory act of December 22, 1775, which forbade all trade with the Colonies, and treated captured property as if it were of enemy ownership. These measures were excused by English partisans as merely being retaliatory in character, and designed to repress the revolt which had already begun in America.[6]

In response to these prohibitions which England undertook to impose on American trade, the Continental Congress on April 6, 1776, opened commerce with American ports to all nations, except Great Britain.[7] This virtually amounted to an implied declaration of independence.[8]

---

[1] Morison, *Sources and Documents illustrating the American Revolution*, 199.

[2] John Dickinson, *Letters from a Farmer*, 8, 20. Indeed, it was an economic burden inflicted by law, as is a tax. See Holmes, *Collected Legal Papers*, 173.

[3] Jefferson, *Works*, II, 68–71, 128–29.

[4] 14 Geo. III, c. 19. For debate in Parliament on this act, see Force, *American Archives* (4th series), I, 35–66.

[5] 15 Geo. III, c. 10; 15 Geo. III, c. 18; 16 Geo. III, c. 5. For debate in Parliament on these acts, see Force, *American Archives* (4th series), I, 1622–96, 1697–1719; VI, 186–237. Regarding the act of 16 Geo. III, c. 5, see page 12 above and pages 144–45 below.

[6] Hutchinson, *Strictures*, 22.

[7] *Journals*, IV, 258. Opening of the ports had been advocated as early as February 16, 1776, in a resolution offered by George Wythe. *Ibid.*, VI, 1072. Capture of English ships and privateering had been authorized on March 19, 1776. *Ibid.*, IV, 213–14, 229–32, 251–54. See "Diary of Richard Smith in the Continental Congress, 1775–1776," *American Historical Review*, Vol. I, No. 2 (April, 1896), 502, 511–14.

[8] Adams, *Works*, III, 29–39.

whole to take into their farther consideration
the declaration and after some time the president resumed the chair and Mr Harrison reported
that the committee not having yet gone through
it desired leave to sit again
Resolved That this Congress will to morrow
again resolve itself into a committee of the
whole to take into their farther consideration
the declaration on independence.

Adjourned to 9 o'clock to morrow.

Thursday July 4. 1776.
Resolved That application be made to the committee of safety of Pensylvania for a supply of
flints for the troops at New york; and that
Delaware government and Maryland be
requested to embody their militia for the
flying camp with all possible expedition
and to march them without delay to the city
of Philadelphia

Agreable to the order of the day the Congress resolved itself into a committee of the
whole to take into their farther consideration
the declaration and after some time

The president resumed the chair
Mr Harrison reported that the committee
have

have agreed to a declaration, which they desired him
to report

The Declaration being read was agreed to
as follows.

A Declaration by the representatives of the
united States of America in Congress assembled

When in the course of human events, it becomes necessary for one people to dissolve the political
bands which have connected them with another,
and to assume among the powers of the earth,
the separate and equal station, to which the laws
of nature and of nature's God entitle them a
decent respect to the opinions of mankind
requires that they should declare the causes
which impel them to the separation

We hold these truths to be self evident, That
all men are created equal, that they are endowed
by their creator with equal unalienable rights,
that among these are life, liberty & the pursuit of
happiness; that to secure these rights governments
are instituted among men, deriving their just
powers from the consent of the governed; that
whenever any form of government becomes
destructive of these ends, it is the right of the people
to

Corrected Journal—first page of the Declaration

For *imposing Taxes on us without our Consent:*

Taxation imposed upon Americans without their consent given through their own local legislative bodies was one of the principal grievances which led to the Revolution. Being the best-known charge against the British king and government, little need be said of it here.

The Stamp Act of March 22, 1765, was the signal for a vigorous outbreak of opposition in America.[1] It was repealed on March 18, 1766, but the Declaratory Act passed at the same time claimed the right to legislate for the Colonies "in all cases whatsoever."

Thereafter the Townshend Act of June 29, 1767, was passed, imposing duties on glass, lead, paint, paper, tea, and other articles.[2] John Dickinson's *Letters from a Farmer* were evoked by this legislation, which seemed as dangerous in principle as the Stamp Act. On April 12, 1770, these duties were repealed, except that on tea, as being "contrary to the true principles of commerce" and tending to discourage production and manufacturing in Great Britain.[3]

The Stamp Act Congress on October 19, 1765, declared "That it is inseparably essential to the freedom of a people, and the undoubted rights of Englishmen, that no taxes should be imposed on them, but with their own consent, given personally, or by their representatives," and that "it is unreasonable and inconsistent with the principles and spirit of the British constitution, for the people of Great Britain to grant to his majesty the property of the colonists."[4] The Massachusetts circular letter of February 11, 1768, proclaimed "that it is an essential, unalterable right, in nature, engrafted into the British constitution, as a fundamental law ... that what a man has honestly acquired is absolutely his own, which

[1] The earlier Sugar Act of April 5, 1764, 4 Geo. III, c. 15, provoked opposition in the Colonies and was repealed in 1766, except for the duties on tea. 6 Geo. III, c. 52.

[2] A drawback on tea exported to the Colonies was provided in the act of July 2, 1767, 7 Geo. III, c. 56. Townshend accompanied his revenue act with laws strengthening enforcement by extending the jurisdiction of admiralty courts and providing for customs commissioners in America. See page 116 above and pages 132–33 below.

[3] 10 Geo. III, c. 17.

[4] Niles, *Principles and Acts of the Revolution*, 457.

he may freely give, but cannot be taken from him without his consent."[5]

In similar vein, Dickinson in his *Letters from a Farmer* regarded a tax as a deprivation of property, while regulation of commerce merely prevented the acquisition of property, and was a legitimate exercise of Parliament's function as supreme legislature within the British imperial system.[6] In his petition to the King from the Pennsylvania assembly, he said, on March 9, 1771: "Your Royal Wisdom will perceive that we can call nothing our own, which others assume a Right to take from us, without our consent."[7]

The same theme recurs repeatedly throughout all the writings in which the colonists presented their cause, whether in petitions to king and Parliament, in other state papers, in pamphlets, in private correspondence, or in solemn appeals to the public opinion of mankind such as the Declaration of Independence.

FOR *depriving us, in many Cases, of the Benefits of Trial by Jury:*

The words "in many Cases" were added in Congress.

Trial by jury has never been available in admiralty courts. In like manner, offenses against excise laws and acts of trade were determined without jury in England. An instance of trial for piracy in 1773 in Massachusetts without a jury is recorded in Governor Hutchinson's *History*.[1]

When the Sugar Act of April 5, 1764,[2] entrusted to the courts of admiralty and vice-admiralty the task of enforcing "acts of

[5] *Massachusetts State Papers*, 134. On January 20, 1768, in a letter to their agent in London, the Massachusetts House wrote: "It is an essential, natural right, that a man shall quietly enjoy and have the sole disposal of his own property." *Ibid.*, 124.

[6] Pages 42, 137.

[7] *The Writings of John Dickinson*, 451. The same idea occurs in Locke, *Two Treatises of Government*, 188, and in *Massachusetts State Papers*, 126, 346. See page 60 above.

[1] Hutchinson, *The History of . . . Massachusetts Bay*, III, 417–22; Hutchinson, *Diary*, I, 74–75.

[2] 4 Geo. III, c. 15.

parliament relating to the trade and revenues" of the British Colonies in America, and when the act of 1768[3] increased the number of such courts having jurisdiction of offenses under those laws, the area of trial without a jury was considerably enlarged.[4]

An eminent English legal historian observes that of all the new methods adopted to strengthen the administration of the acts of trade "the most effective, and therefore the most disliked, was the extension given to the jurisdiction of the reorganized courts of admiralty and vice-admiralty. It was the most effective, because it deprived the defendant of the right to be tried by a jury which was almost certain not to convict him."[5]

Penalties for smuggling imposed by judges dependent on the crown, without the benefit of possible acquittal by a sympathetic jury, presented a very painful prospect, and the colonists were vigorous in their protests against those acts to "extend the powers of the admiralty courts beyond their ancient limits."[6]

For *transporting us beyond Seas to be tried for pretended Offences:*

The expression "pretended Offences" was used by Jefferson in his draft of the *Declaration on Taking up Arms.*[1]

Americans could be transported "beyond Seas" as witnesses, under the so-called act "for the impartial administration of justice" in Massachusetts,[2] if their attendance was desired by either prosecutor or defendant in prosecutions against persons charged with murder for acts done in the suppression of riots or in the enforcement of the revenue laws.

Moreover, defendants in revenue cases under 4 Geo. III, c. 15 and 8 Geo. III, c. 22 might be tried in vice-admiralty courts not located in the colony where the offense was committed. Thus

[3] 8 Geo. III, c. 22. See page 116 above.

[4] Lind, *An Answer to the Declaration,* 70; Hutchinson, *Strictures,* 24.

[5] Holdsworth, *A History of English Law,* XI, 110.

[6] Resolutions of October 14, 1774, in the first Continental Congress, *Journals,* I, 71; Massachusetts Resolves of June 29, 1769, *Massachusetts State Papers,* 179, 307; Resolutions of Stamp Act Congress, October 19, 1765, Niles, *Principles and Acts of the Revolution,* 457.

[1] *Works,* II, 116.

[2] See page 127 above.

a seizure made in Georgia could be tried in Halifax, fifteen hundred miles away.[3]

Americans could also be transported to England for trial themselves as defendants in the case of certain offenses against the king's property. An act passed on April 16, 1772,[4] prescribed the penalty of death "if any person or persons shall, either within this realm, or in any of the islands, countries, forts, or places thereunto belonging, wilfully and maliciously set on fire, or burn, or otherwise destroy . . . any of his Majesty's ships or vessels of war . . . or any of his Majesty's arsenals, magazines, dock yards, rope yards, victualling offices, or any of the buildings erected therein, or belonging thereto; or any timber or materials there placed, for building, repairing, or fitting out of ships or vessels; or any of his Majesty's military, naval, or victualling stores, or other ammunition of war, or any place or places, where any such military, naval, or victualling stores, or other ammunition of war, is, are, or shall be kept placed, or deposited."

With respect to the place of trial, the act further provided "That any person who shall commit any of the offences before mentioned, in any place out of this realm, may be indicted and tried for the same, either in any shire or county within this realm, in like manner and form, as if such offence had been committed within the said shire or county, or in such island, country, or place, where such offence shall have been actually committed, as his Majesty, his heirs, or successors, may deem most expedient for bringing such offender to justice; any law, usage, or custom notwithstanding."

This act was included among the objectionable Parliamentary legislation against which protest was made by the first Continental Congress in its resolutions of October 14, 1774.[5] The act was passed before the schooner *Gaspee,* an offensive revenue craft, was burned by a mob in Narragansett Bay on June 10, 1772, but did not become known to the people in America until after that incident.[6]

[3] Washburne, *Imperial Control of the Administration of Justice,* 177. See page 116 above.

[4] 12 Geo. III, c. 24; Lind, *An Answer to the Declaration,* 75-77.

[5] *Journals,* I, 72. See also, regarding the *Gaspee* court, *ibid.,* 97.

[6] Hutchinson, *Strictures,* 25. Cf. Lind, *An Answer to the Declaration,* 77.

Following the *Gaspee* incident, a royal court of inquiry was constituted by a commission dated September 2, 1772. It was composed of the governor of Rhode Island, the chief justices of New Jersey and Massachusetts, and Judge Robert Auchmuty of the vice-admiralty court in Boston. The third article of the court's instructions, dated September 4, 1772, directed that persons found to be implicated should be delivered to the naval commander in chief to be sent to England for trial. The court submitted its report under date of June 22, 1773, but found the evidence insufficient to enable it to apprehend any of the culprits involved.[7]

The court of inquiry into the *Gaspee* incident was mentioned in a circular letter of June 3, 1773, from the Massachusetts House to the speakers of other assemblies, and caused considerable concern in Virginia.[8] On March 12, 1773, the Virginia Committee of Correspondence was directed to inquire particularly into this matter.[9]

Another law under which Americans faced the danger of being tried in England, particularly as a result of riots in Boston, was an old statute against treason enacted in 1543 during the reign of Henry VIII.[10] That act provided "That all manner of offences, being already made and declared, or hereafter to be made or declared by any of the laws and statutes of this realm to be treasons, misprisions of treasons, or concealments of treasons, and done perpetrated or committed, or hereafter to be done, perpetrated, or committed, by any person or persons out of this realm of England, shall be from henceforth enquired of, heard and determined before the King's justices of his bench, for pleas to be holden before himself, by good and lawful men of the same shire where the said bench shall sit and be kept, or else before such commissioners, and in such shire of the realm, as shall be assigned

[7] William R. Staples, *The Documentary History of the Destruction of the Gaspee*, 22, 52–54.

[8] *Massachusetts State Papers*, 401; Jefferson, *Works* I, 9.

[9] *Journals of the House of Burgesses of Virginia 1773–1776*, 28. The assembly was prorogued because of an address two days earlier protesting against the trial of some counterfeiters outside the county where they were apprehended or the crime was committed. *Ibid.*, 22.

[10] 35 Henry VIII, c. 2. See Holdsworth, *A History of English Law*, XI, 114; Wells, *Life and Public Services of Samuel Adams*, I, 209, 228, 235–37; Hosmer, *Life of Thomas Hutchinson*, 243; Hutchinson, *Diary*, I, 219.

by the king's majesty's commission, and by good and lawful men of the same shire, in like manner and form to all intents and purposes, as if such treasons, misprisions of treasons, or concealments of treasons had been done, perpetrated and committed within the same shire where they shall be so enquired of, heard and determined as is aforesaid."

The Duke of Bedford on December 15, 1768, in the House of Lords, moved an address to the King, requesting that the governor of Massachusetts be directed to make an investigation and obtain evidence regarding the events in Boston "in order that your Majesty may issue a special commission for enquiring of, hearing, and determining the said offences within this realm, pursuant to the provisions of the statute of the 35th year of the reign of king Henry the eighth, in case your Majesty shall, upon receiving the said information, see sufficient ground for such a proceeding." This address was agreed to by both branches of Parliament, in spite of strenuous opposition in the House of Commons by Burke, Barré, and other champions of American rights.[11]

Lord Camden in 1775 attacked the ministry for wishing to bring Americans overseas under the act of Henry VIII to be "butchered" in the court of king's bench. Regarding the effect of this ancient statute, in conjunction with the act for "impartial" administration of justice in Massachusetts, he declared: "If an American kills an Englishman, he is dragged hither, far from his neighbours, his friends, his witnesses; from all possibility of vindicating his innocence. If an Englishman kills an American, he is brought home to his own country, to be tried with all advantages, and without testimony or circumstances to prove his guilt."[12] Other opponents of the use of the act of Henry VIII argued from its history and the circumstances surrounding its enactment that it was not appropriately applicable to the Colonies.[13]

In connection with discussions of that statute, the Virginia House of Burgesses was dissolved for resolutions of May 16, 1769, declaring that the sole power of imposing taxes was in the House of Burgesses and that all trials for treason, misprision of

[11] *Parliamentary History*, XVI, 476, 479–80, 510.
[12] *Ibid.*, XVIII, 292, 440.
[13] *Ibid.*, XVI, 507–10; XVIII, 524.

treason, or for any felony or crime whatsoever ought of right to be conducted in courts within the colony.[14]

The first Continental Congress on October 21, 1774, adopted a resolution declaring "That the seizing, or attempting to seize, any person in America, in order to transport such person beyond the sea, for trial of offences, committed within the body of a county in America, being against law, will justify, and ought to meet with resistance and reprisal."[15]

FOR *abolishing the free System of English Laws in a neighbouring Province, establishing therein an arbitrary Government, and enlarging its Boundaries, so as to render it at once an Example and fit Instrument for introducing the same absolute Rule into these Colonies:*

This charge was added by the committee. It does not appear in the Adams copy, and was inserted by Jefferson as an interlineation at the bottom of the second page of the Rough Draft. The word "Colonies" was restored by Congress, Jefferson or a member of the committee having changed it to "states."

This grievance arose from the Quebec Act of June 22, 1774.[1] That act was mentioned in the resolutions of the first Continental Congress.[2] It provided that the boundaries of Quebec, as proclaimed in 1763, should be extended to include all the country west of the Alleghenies and south to the Ohio River.[3] This would hamper westward migration, and curtail the territory governed by the common law under free institutions, while extending the area where Roman law would prevail.

[14] *Journals of the House of Burgesses of Virginia 1766-1769*, 214-15, 218.

[15] *Journals*, I, 102.

[1] 14 Geo. III, c. 83. For debate in Parliament on this act, see Force, *American Archives* (4th series), I, 169-220.

[2] *Journals*, I, 72.

[3] Friedenwald, *The Declaration of Independence*, 250; Hutchinson, *Strictures*, 25-26.

FOR *taking away our Charters, abolishing our most valuable Laws, and altering fundamentally the Forms of our Governments:*

Franklin inserted in committee the words "abolishing our most
valuable Laws." I think the word "valuable" is in Jefferson's handwriting, Franklin having originally written "important."

The Massachusetts Government Act of 1774 is the foremost
instance of altering a form of government established by charter.[1]
The principal change made by that act was in the mode of select-
ing juries and the appointment and tenure of the Council.[2] The
Council had been elected by the House, but under the act it was
to be appointed by the crown. The sheriff was likewise to be appointed by the crown, and juries were to be chosen by him instead
of being elected.

When Governor Hutchinson turned over the provincial garrison at Castle William to British regulars, and when he and the
judges accepted salaries from the crown instead of depending on
grants by the assembly, the patriotic party claimed that the charter was being disregarded.[3] His removal of the assembly from
Boston to Cambridge pursuant to instructions from England was
also regarded as an infraction of the charter.[4] The attempt of the
governor of North Carolina to establish courts without authority
of law might also have been in mind when this provision of the
Declaration was drafted.[5]

This grievance was seriously felt by the colonists. If charters
of government can be disregarded, what is safe? English writers
pointed out that most charters were themselves nothing but acts
repealing prior charters.[6] The colonists, however, regarded charters as fundamental law. Hence, relying on the doctrines of

[1] Hutchinson, *Strictures*, 26.

[2] Lind, *An Answer to the Declaration*, 88–89.

[3] *Massachusetts State Papers*, 259, 324–29, 397.

[4] Hutchinson, *History of . . . Massachusetts Bay*, III, 302, 366, 345.

[5] Friedenwald, *The Declaration of Independence*, 233, 253.

[6] Lind, *An Answer to the Declaration*, 82.

Vattel[7] and Locke,[8] they considered disregard of the charter as subversive of government.[9]

FOR *suspending our own Legislatures, and declaring themselves invested with Power to legislate for us in all Cases whatsoever.*

The corrected Journal omits the word "own." This is an error in copying.

The charge of "suspending our own Legislatures" refers to the act of June 15, 1767 (7 Geo. III, c. 59), affecting the legislature of New York. Because provision to maintain British troops was not made by New York in exact accordance with English statutes, this act suspended its legislative powers until such action was taken.

Parliament directed that from and after October 1, 1767, "until provision shall have been made by the said assembly of *New York* for furnishing his Majesty's troops within the said province with all such necessaries as are required by the said acts of parliament, or any of them, to be furnished for such troops, it shall not be lawful for the governor . . . to pass, or give his . . . assent to, or concurrence in, the making or passing of any act of assembly . . . order, resolution, or vote," or for the House of Representatives "to pass or make any bill, order, resolution or vote of any kind, for any other purpose whatsoever" (except for adjournment or election of a speaker).

The British legislature further ordained that "all acts of assembly, orders, resolutions, and votes whatsoever which shall or may be passed, assented to, or made, contrary to the tenor and meaning of this act," in New York after October 1, 1767, "before and until provision shall have been made for supplying his Majesty's troops with necessaries as aforesaid, shall be, and are hereby declared to be, null and void, and of no force or effect whatsoever."

[7] *The Law of Nations*, III, 19 (Book I, chap. iii, § 34).
[8] *Two Treatises of Government*, 225–26.
[9] *Massachusetts State Papers*, 134, 395.

However, the New York assembly by an act of June 6, 1767, had granted £3,000 for the troops. Deeming that this constituted compliance with the requirements of the Suspending Act, the legislature continued to function after that act was officially communicated to it on November 18, 1767. The validity of its proceedings after the date when the suspension act took effect was upheld by a British order in council of August 12, 1768.[1]

Jefferson in his *Summary View* comments with spirit upon this grievance: "One free and independent legislature hereby takes upon itself to suspend the powers of another, free and independent as itself. . . . Not only the principles of common sense, but the common feelings of human nature, must be surrendered up before his majesty's subjects here can be persuaded to believe that they hold their political existence at the will of a British parliament. Shall these governments be dissolved, their property annihilated, and their people reduced to a state of nature, at the imperious breath of a body of men, whom they never saw, in whom they never confided, and over whom they have no powers of punishment or removal, let their crimes against the American public be ever so great?"[2]

Parliament claimed the power to legislate for the Colonies "in all cases whatsoever" in the Declaratory Act of 1766, which it passed at the time it repealed the Stamp Act.[3] Protest against the Declaratory Act was made in the resolutions of October 14, 1774, of the first Continental Congress, and in the *Declaration on Taking up Arms* adopted by the second Continental Congress on July 6, 1775.[4] The language in Jefferson's draft of the latter paper is very similar to the passage which appears in the Declaration of Independence:

But why should we enumerate their injuries in detail? By one act they have suspended the powers of one American legislature, & by another have declared they may legislate for us themselves

[1] Lind, *An Answer to the Declaration*, 91; *The Colonial Laws of New York*, IV, 947–51; *Documents Relative to the Colonial History of the State of New-York*, VIII, 63–64, 88–91. See page 127 above.

[2] Page 12.

[3] See page 4 above.

[4] *Journals*, I, 64; II, 146.

in all cases whatsoever. These two acts alone form a basis broad enough whereon to erect a despotism of unlimited extent.[5]

DEEDS OF VIOLENCE AND CRUELTY

HE *has abdicated Government here, by declaring us out of his Protection and waging War against us.*

The Rough Draft reads:

He has abdicated government here, withdrawing his governors, & declaring us out of his allegiance & protection.

The amendment was made by Congress.

Here the Declaration resumes its charges against the King alone, having concluded the enumeration of the "acts of pretended legislation" in which the King had "combined" with "others."

The reference here is to the proclamation of August 23, 1775, declaring the existence of rebellion, and the speech from the throne of October 26, 1775.[1]

Governors Dunmore of Virginia, Tryon of New York, Martin of North Carolina, and Campbell of South Carolina, abdicated government in 1775.[2] Governor Dunmore's flight to the *Fowey* has previously been described.[3] A similar attempt was made by Governor Tryon to carry on the public business while aboard the Halifax packet.[4] Governor Martin, also, reduced to being a tame spectator of rebellion, spent over fourteen months on board ship after fleeing from a mob and witnessing the burning of Fort Johnston by the courageous John Ashe under the very eyes of the *Cruizer* where the Governor had taken refuge.[5] According

[5] *Ibid.*, II, 133; Jefferson, *Works*, II, 117.

[1] Force, *American Archives* (4th series), III, 240–41; VI, 1–3. See pages 11–12 above.

[2] Friedenwald, *The Declaration of Independence*, 255.

[3] See page 101 above.

[4] *Documents Relative to the Colonial History of the State of New-York*, VIII, 640–41.

[5] *The Colonial Records of North Carolina*, X, 41–50, 96–98, 108–109, 174, 232, 247–48, 407, 735.

to English precedent, such abandonment of public duty warrants the choice of new rulers by representatives of the people.[6]

HE *has plundered our Seas, ravaged our Coasts, burnt our Towns, and destroyed the Lives of our People.*

This charge refers to the burning of Falmouth, Charlestown, Norfolk, and Charleston by the British.[1] The circumstances here enumerated amount in substance merely to a statement that war was actually being waged, with its customary incidents of cruelty and devastation, by a ruler against his people. War is always evil, and the source of other evils; but perhaps Jefferson, no militarist himself, believed that the hostilities being conducted in America by the English were marked by extraordinary atrocity; or perhaps he regarded it as a supreme outrage that a king should lift his sword against his own subjects, merely because they were "opposing with manly firmness his invasions on the rights of the people."

Former royal Governor Hutchinson of Massachusetts, on the other hand, considered that it was only natural for war to be waged, with all its attendant harshness and ferocity, in case of rebellion such as that existing in America.[2]

HE *is, at this Time, transporting large Armies of foreign Mercenaries to compleat the Works of Death, Desolation, and Tyranny, already begun with circumstances of Cruelty and Perfidy, scarcely paralleled in the most barbarous Ages, and totally unworthy the Head of a civilized Nation.*

[6] The English Bill of Rights of December 16, 1689, recited that King James II had abdicated government. 1 Wm. and Mary, 2 sess., c. 2, in George B. Adams and H. M. Stephens, *Select Documents of English Constitutional History*, 463. Locke also considers it a dissolution of government "When he who has the supreme executive power neglects and abandons that charge." *Two Treatises of Government*, 227.

[1] Friedenwald, *The Declaration of Independence*, 255. Capture of trading ships was authorized by the act of December 22, 1775. 16 Geo. III, c. 5.

[2] *Strictures*, 28. Countercharges were made against the Americans. Lind, *An Answer to the Declaration*, 99–100.

On May 21, 1776, Congress learned definitely that foreign mercenary troops had been hired by George III and were on their way to America. A communication from General Washington confirming earlier reports on this subject was read on that day. Copies of treaties were enclosed, which George III had made with the German principalities of Hesse-Cassel, Brunswick, and Hanau whereby they were to furnish troops for Britain's battles with the colonists. Holland and Russia had refused to supply any soldiers for this purpose.[1]

Jefferson was a member of the committee charged by Congress with the responsibility of giving publicity to this news, and of considering "an adequate reward for the person who brought the intelligence." He also served on a committee to prepare measures for encouraging desertion by the Hessians, as the German mercenaries were commonly called.[2] The information received by Congress was published in the *Pennsylvania Gazette* of May 22, 1776, and in other newspapers. It incensed the populace and contributed greatly to the rising tide of sentiment in favor of independence.

In resenting the use of Hessians, the colonists were reflecting the traditional English attitude toward the military prerogatives of the king. Considerable concern was felt in Parliament regarding the employment of foreign troops,[3] and there was opposition when the ministry announced that treaties had been concluded for the purpose of sending mercenaries to America.[4]

HE *has constrained our fellow Citizens taken Captive on the high Seas to bear Arms against their Country, to become the Executioners of their Friends and Brethren, or to fall themselves by their Hands.*

[1] Washington, *Writings*, V, 56. See also *ibid.*, IV, 409–10; V, 22–23; Force, *American Archives* (4th series), V, 1184–86; *Journals*, IV, 341. Letters were read in Congress on May 10 dealing with a request by Massachusetts for reinforcements because it was reported that twelve thousand Hessians were bound for Boston.

[2] *Journals*, IV, 369–70; V, 640, 653.

[3] *Parliamentary History*, XVIII, 798–841. This instance involved use of troops from Hanover to garrison Gibraltar and Minorca.

[4] *Ibid.*, 1156–88.

This passage was inserted in committee and transposed in Congress. It was originally placed immediately after a paragraph which was stricken out by Congress, reading: "He has incited treasonable insurrections of our fellow-citizens, with the allurements of forfeiture & confiscation of our property." That paragraph followed the charge relating to Indian warfare.

This charge refers to the act of Parliament of December 22, 1775 (16 Geo. III, c. 5), which in addition to authorizing capture of vessels and cargoes trading with America "as if the same were the ships and effects of open enemies," empowered the captors "to cause to be taken, or put on board any other ships or vessels, all and every the masters, crews, and other persons, who shall be found on board such . . . ships as shall be seized and taken as prize as aforesaid; and also to enter the names of such of the said mariners and crews, upon the book or books of his Majesty's said ships or vessels, as they . . . shall . . . think fit."

The victims thus compelled to participate in naval warfare against their own countrymen were declared by the act "to be as much in the service of his Majesty, to all intents and purposes, as if the said mariners and crews had entered themselves voluntarily to serve on board his Majesty's said ships and vessels respectively."

Persons on board whom the captors did not see fit to enroll for naval service could be detained until arrival at a port in Great Britain, Ireland, or a part of America not in rebellion, and there set at liberty on shore.

As has been noted above,[1] the act of December 22, 1775, was one of the causes which contributed substantially toward hastening the advent of independence. To be treated by the King as if they were "open enemies" went far to convince Americans that they could not at the same time continue to be his loyal subjects. This act was referred to in the resolutions of May 15, 1776, by which the Virginia Convention directed its delegation in Congress to propose independence.

Opponents of this measure in England had anticipated its evil consequences. The Duke of Richmond, during debate in the House of Lords, remarked that "this bill is a formal denuncia-

[1] See pages 12 and 122 above.

tion of war against the Colonies." Moreover, by indiscriminately subjecting loyalists to the same penalties as rebels, it would produce unanimity of action among Americans. "I do not think the people of *America* in rebellion, but resisting acts of the most unexampled cruelty and oppression," he exclaimed, amidst disorder and tumultuous charges that his language was unparliamentary and unpatriotic.

Particularly objectionable was the provision treating captured seamen as if they had voluntarily enlisted in the British navy. This meant that, unlike other victims of impressment, they were punishable with death for desertion. With forceful eloquence the Duke declared that "you compel them to fight against their fathers, brothers, and nearest relatives; and that, too, contrary to the conviction of their own conscience; and should they refuse to execute the barbarous service with rigour and punctuality, you are then authorized . . . to shoot them for a breach of duty."

In like vein the protest of the dissenting lords who voted against the bill recorded that "we reject, with indignation, that clause . . . which, by a refinement in tyranny, and in a sentence worse than death, obliges the unhappy men who shall be made captives in this predatory war, to bear arms against their family, kindred, friends, and country; and after being plundered themselves, to become accomplices in plundering their brethren."[2]

Impressment of American seamen to serve on British ships continued to be a long-standing grievance for many years after the Declaration of Independence. Controversy between the two nations regarding this practice persisted until the War of 1812. Jefferson, while president, refused to submit to the Senate a treaty with England negotiated by Monroe, because it did not contain a provision prohibiting impressment.[3]

HE *has excited domestic Insurrections amongst us, and has endeavoured to bring on the Inhabitants of our Frontiers, the merciless Indian Savages, whose known Rule of Warfare, is an undistinguished Destruction, of all Ages, Sexes and Conditions.*

[2] Force, *American Archives* (4th series), VI, 215–17, 227.
[3] Jefferson, *Works*, XI, 13.

The words "excited domestic Insurrections amongst us, and has" were inserted in Congress.

This amendment preserved the substance of the paragraph, deleted by Congress, which came next in the Rough Draft: "He has incited treasonable insurrections of our fellow-citizens, with the allurements of forfeiture & confiscation of our property."

The omitted paragraph was followed in the Rough Draft by the paragraph on impressment of seamen, which was transposed by Congress and placed after the paragraph about foreign mercenaries.

Following this transposed paragraph, the Rough Draft contained a lengthy and rhetorical condemnation of the slave trade, which concluded and brought to a highly wrought climax the charges against the King. This passage, which was rejected in its entirety by Congress, reads:

He has waged cruel war against human nature itself, violating it's most sacred rights of life & liberty in the persons of a distant people who never offended him, captivating & carrying them into slavery in another hemisphere, or to incur miserable death in their transportation thither. This piratical warfare, the opprobrium of infidel *powers, is the warfare of the* Christian *king of Great Britain. Determined to keep open a market where MEN should be bought & sold, he has prostituted his negative for suppressing every legislative attempt to prohibit or to restrain this execrable commerce: and that this assemblage of horrors might want no fact of distinguished die, he is now exciting those very people to rise in arms among us, and to purchase that liberty of which* he *has deprived them, by murdering the people upon whom* he *also obtruded them; thus paying off former crimes committed against the* liberties *of one people, with crimes which he urges them to commit against the* lives *of another.*

As John Adams had anticipated, this "vehement philippic" was not palatable either to Southern slaveowners, or to New England traders.

English encouragement to slave and Indian revolts is here referred to. Lord Dunmore in 1775 threatened a slave insurrec-

146

The Parchment Declaration in 1950

tion in Virginia. It was reported to the House of Burgesses "that his Lordship swore by the living God that if . . . any Injury or insult were offered to himself . . . he would declare Freedom to the Slaves, and reduce the City of *Williamsburg* to Ashes."[1] The governors of North Carolina and South Carolina were known to be planning a similar uprising. General Gage in the summer of 1775 tried to get Indian allies. An English agent named Stuart won over Creeks and Chickasaws on the borders of South Carolina. Sir Guy Carleton made some progress in negotiations with the Six Nations.[2]

The danger of Indian attacks, incited by British agents, remained a constant menace for many years after the close of the Revolution. England did not evacuate the western posts as required by the peace treaty of September 3, 1783, claiming that their retention was justified because of American failure to pay the debts due to English merchants before the war. Jefferson's able arguments defending the American position while secretary of state in the administration of President George Washington were frustrated by the pro-British machinations of his cabinet colleague Alexander Hamilton. The controversy was not disposed of until Jay's Treaty of November 19, 1794.[3]

[1] *Journals of the House of Burgesses of Virginia 1773–1776*, 231. For his proclamation of November 7, 1775, declaring martial law and freeing slaves who joined the King's troops, see Force, *American Archives* (4th series), III, 1385.

[2] Friedenwald, *The Declaration of Independence*, 256–57. English partisans claimed that the Americans first used Indians in the war. Lind, *An Answer to the Declaration*, 108.

[3] Andrew C. McLaughlin, "The Western Posts and the British Debts," *Annual Report of the American Historical Association for the Year 1894*, 413–44; Samuel F. Bemis, *Jay's Treaty: A Study in Commerce and Diplomacy*, 102, 106, 200; Jefferson to the British minister, George Hammond, Philadelphia, May 29, 1792, Jefferson, *Works*, VII, 3–98.

Vain Appeals to British King and People

In *every stage of these Oppressions we have Petitioned for Redress in the most humble Terms: Our repeated Petitions have been answered only by repeated Injury. A Prince, whose Character is thus marked by every act which may define a Tyrant, is unfit to be the Ruler of a free People.*

Congress substituted the words "a free People" for "a people who mean to be free," and deleted the following additional sentence:

Future ages will scarce believe that the hardiness of one man, adventured within the short compass of twelve years only, on so many acts of tyranny without a mask, over a people fostered & fixed in principles of liberty.

The Declaration now refers to the repeated petitions and remonstrances made by the colonists.[1] John Dickinson was most insistent on the exhaustion of this procedure prior to independence. Such cautious advance annoyed less timid patriots such as Jefferson and Adams.[2] But the English did not consider as "humble" petitions the colonists' declarations that the power of Parliament and prerogatives of the crown were grievances.[3]

That the King was a tyrant, even in the sense in which Locke used the term, was denied by former Governor Hutchinson of Massachusetts: "Have these men given an instance of any one Act in which the King has exceeded the just Powers of the Crown as limited by the English Constitution? Has he ever departed from known established laws, and substituted his own will as the rule of his action?"[4]

[1] Petitions to the King were adopted by the first and second Continental Congresses on October 26, 1774, and July 8, 1775. *Journals*, I, 115–21; II, 158–61. The individual colonies had also petitioned separately. Jefferson, *Works*, II, 106.

[2] Jefferson, *Works*, I, 19.

[3] Lind, *An Answer to the Declaration*, 112.

[4] *Strictures*, 30. See page 85 above.

A free people, as defined by Dickinson, was one whose government was so constructed as to prevent the exercise of arbitrary power. "For who are a free people? Not those over whom government is reasonably and equitably exercised, but those who live under a government so constitutionally checked and controlled that proper provision is made against its ever being otherwise exercised."[5] Elsewhere Dickinson says that the freedom of a people consists in their being governed by laws in which no change can be made without their consent.[6]

NOR *have we been wanting in Attentions to our British Brethren. We have warned them from Time to Time of Attempts by their Legislature to extend an unwarrantable Jurisdiction over us. We have reminded them of the Circumstances of our Emigration and Settlement here. We have appealed to their native Justice and Magnanimity, and we have conjured them by the Ties of our common Kindred to disavow these Usurpations, which, would inevitably interrupt our Connections and Correspondence. They too have been deaf to the Voice of Justice and of Consanguinity. We must, therefore, acquiesce in the Necessity, which denounces our Separation, and hold them, as we hold the rest of Mankind, Enemies in War, in Peace, Friends.*

The corrected Journal omits the word "of" before "Consanguinity." This is an error in copying.

In the Rough Draft this paragraph reads:

"*Nor have we been wanting in attentions to our British brethren. We have warned them from time to time of attempts by their legislature to extend a jurisdiction over these our states. We have reminded them of the circumstances of our emigration & settlement here, no one of which could warrant so strange a pretension: that*

[5] Stillé, *The Life and Times of John Dickinson*, 89.
[6] *The Political Writings of John Dickinson*, I, 403.

149

these were effected at the expence of our own blood & treasure, unassisted by the wealth or the strength of Great Britain: that in constituting indeed our several forms of government, we had adopted one common king, thereby laying a foundation for perpetual league & amity with them: but that submission to their parliament was no part of our constitution, nor ever in idea, if history may be credited: and we appealed to their native justice & magnanimity, as well as to the ties of our common kindred to disavow these usurpations which were likely to interrupt our correspondence & connection. They too have been deaf to the voice of justice & of consanguinity, & when occasions have been given them, by the regular course of their laws, of removing from their councils the disturbers of our harmony, they have by their free election re-established them in power. At this very time too they are permitting their chief magistrate to send over not only soldiers of our common blood, but Scotch & foreign mercenaries to invade & deluge us in blood. These facts have given the last stab to agonizing affection and manly spirit bids us to renounce forever these unfeeling brethren. We must endeavor to forget our former love for them, and to hold them as we hold the rest of mankind, enemies in war, in peace friends. We might have been a free & a great people together; but a communication of grandeur & of freedom it seems is below their dignity. Be it so, since they will have it: the road to glory & happiness is open to us too; we will climb it in a separate state, and acquiesce in the necessity which pronounces our everlasting Adieu!"

Jefferson amended the last sentence to read: "the road to happiness & to glory is open to us too; we will climb it apart from them, and acquiesce in the necessity which denounces our eternal separation." Besides other alterations made by Congress before deleting the whole paragraph, the second sentence was changed to read "attempts by their legislature to extend an unwarrantable jurisdiction over us."

It will be noted that Congress deleted all reference to Parliament, as well as the passages criticizing the English people and referring to "Scotch and other foreign mercenaries."

This refers to appeals to the people of England repeatedly made by the Continental Congress.[1]

Likewise, in an address to Governor Dunmore written by Jefferson for the Virginia House of Burgesses, he exclaimed: "For ourselves, we have exhausted every mode of application which our invention could suggest as proper and promising. We have decently remonstrated with Parliament: they have added new injuries to the old. We have wearied our King with applications: he has not deigned to answer us. We have appealed to the native honour and justice of the British Nation. Their efforts in our favour have been hitherto ineffectual."[2]

the Circumstances of our Emigration and Settlement here

In language which Congress deleted from Jefferson's original version of the Declaration, Jefferson had elaborated his theory concerning the "circumstances of our emigration and settlement here." He contended that the power of the crown in the Colonies was based on their voluntary adoption of a common chief magistrate.

The same subject Jefferson discussed at length in his *Summary View*. He concludes this discussion with a striking passage: "America was conquered, and her settlements made, and firmly established, at the expense of individuals, and not of the British public. Their own blood was spilt in acquiring lands for their settlement, their own fortunes expended in making that settlement effectual; for themselves they fought, for themselves they conquered, and for themselves alone they have a right to hold. Not a shilling was ever issued from the public treasures of his majesty, or his ancestors, for their assistance, till of very late times, after the colonies had become established on a firm and permanent footing."[1] As he wrote on another occasion, "For us, not for them, has government been instituted here."[2]

[1] Addresses to the people of Great Britain were adopted on October 21, 1774, and July 8, 1775. *Journals*, I, 82–90; II, 163–70.

[2] *Works*, II, 106.

[1] Page 6. See also Jefferson, *Papers*, I, 277–84.

[2] *Works*, II, 102.

Jefferson regarded the settlements in America as new societies, which possessed inherent legislative powers and the right to govern themselves; by their agreement and consent they adopted the common law of England as their own law, and the king of England as their common sovereign.[3]

On the other hand, Governor Hutchinson of Massachusetts viewed the powers of the provincial government as grants from the crown, rather than viewing the powers of the crown as granted by the people of the province. He considered the charters not as compacts or treaties, but as acts of domestic legislation creating municipal corporations.[4]

In similar vein, a modern scholar says that Jefferson's theory rested upon "a patent misconception of historical facts" but harmonized so perfectly with popular sentiment that "nothing else could have served the purpose so well."[5]

The first Continental Congress in its declaration of rights of October 14, 1774, asserted on behalf of the colonists that their ancestors were entitled to all the rights of "free and natural-born subjects, within the realm of England" and had not "forfeited, surrendered, or lost any of those rights" by their emigration to America.[6]

[3] *Summary View*, 6–7. See also page 121 above.

[4] *Massachusetts State Papers*, 333.

[5] Max Farrand, *The Development of the United States*, 44. See also John Quincy Adams, *Memoirs*, VIII, 279, 284.

[6] *Journals*, I, 68.

Assumption of Status of Independent States

WE, therefore, the Representatives of the UNITED
STATES OF AMERICA, *in* General Congress, *Assembled,
appealing to the Supreme Judge of the World for the Rectitude of our Intentions, do, in the Name, and by Authority of
the good People of these Colonies, solemnly Publish and
Declare, That these United Colonies are, and of Right ought
to be,* Free and Independent States; *that they are absolved
from all Allegiance to the British Crown, and that all political
Connection between them and the State of Great-Britain, is
and ought to be totally dissolved; and that as* Free and Independent States, *they have full Power to levy War, conclude Peace, contract Alliances, establish Commerce, and to
do all other Acts and Things which* Independent States *may
of right do. And for the support of this Declaration, with a firm
Reliance on the Protection of divine Providence, we mutually
pledge to each other our Lives, our Fortunes, and our sacred
Honor.*

The Congress, very appropriately, altered the language of this
paragraph of the Declaration so as to make it correspond with the
Lee resolution of independence adopted on July 2, 1776. Jefferson's
Rough Draft had read:

*We therefore the representatives of the United States of Ameri-
ca in General Congress assembled do, in the name & by authority
of the good people of these states, reject and renounce all allegiance
& subjection to the kings of Great Britain & all others who may
hereafter claim by, through, or under them; we utterly dissolve &
break off all political connection which may have heretofore sub-
sisted between us & the people or parliament of Great Britain; and*

153

*finally we do assert and declare these colonies to be free and inde-
pendent states, and that as free & independent states they shall
hereafter have full power to levy war, conclude peace, contract
alliances, establish commerce, & to do all other acts and things
which independent states may of right do. And for the support of
this declaration we mutually pledge to each other our lives, our
fortunes, & our sacred honour.*

Congress also changed "states" to "Colonies," and inserted
two phrases: "appealing to the Supreme Judge of the World for
the Rectitude of our Intentions," and 'with a firm Reliance on the
Protection of divine Providence."

Free and Independent States

Here the Colonies declare themselves subjects of international law. Not only is connection with the crown cut off, but "all
political connection between them and the State of Great Britain."
This language is broad enough to sever any relationship with
Parliament, though the colonists maintained the view that their
connection with Great Britain was solely through the crown. The
Declaration nowhere expressly refers to Parliament by name.
The Virginia instructions pursuant to which Richard Henry Lee
offered his resolutions of independence did mention Parliament,
and Jefferson's Rough Draft speaks of it two times.

Claiming all the powers of sovereign states under international law, the Declaration specifies the powers of war, peace,
foreign affairs, and commerce; these are substantially the powers
assigned to the central government both under the actual practice
of the eighteenth-century British Empire and under the Constitution of the United States.

Advocates of independence had long argued that until separation from England was proclaimed, diplomatic and commercial
relations with foreign nations would be impossible. This was
forcefully stated in the following passage of Paine's *Common
Sense*:

Were a manifesto to be published, and dispatched to foreign
Courts, setting forth the miseries we have endured, and the peace-

able methods we have ineffectually used for redress, declaring at the same time, that not being able any longer to live happily or safely under the cruel disposition of the British Court, we had been driven to the necessity of breaking off all connections with her; at the same time, assuring all such Courts, of our peaceable disposition towards them, and of our desire of entering into trade with them: such a memorial would produce more good effects to this Continent, than if a ship were freighted with petitions to Britain.[1]

Paine could hardly have desired a more effective "manifesto" or "memorial" than that which came a few months later in the Declaration of Independence.

our Lives, our Fortunes, and our sacred Honor

With this solemn conclusion of the Declaration should be compared the striking words of President Woodrow Wilson's message recommending a declaration of war with Germany in 1917: "To such a task we can dedicate our lives and our fortunes, everything that we are and everything that we have, with the pride of those who know that the day has come when America is privileged to spend her blood and her might for the principles that gave her birth and happiness and the peace which she has cherished. God helping her, she can do no other."[1]

When the colonists spoke of their "lives and fortunes,"[2] they were expressing, with eighteenth-century elegance, their willingness to submit to the hardships of military service and taxation.

Signed by ORDER and in BEHALF of the CONGRESS,

JOHN HANCOCK, PRESIDENT.
ATTEST.
CHARLES THOMSON, SECRETARY.

[1] Page 78; Jefferson, *Works*, I, 26–27.

[1] Address to Congress, April 2, 1917.

[2] The words were used repeatedly in New England in 1776 prior to the Declaration of Independence. Hazelton, *The Declaration of Independence*, 53, 390.

The authentication and signature of the original official text of the Declaration, and the signing of the engrossed copy by members of Congress, have been discussed in the section "Texts of the Declaration" and are treated in detail by Chamberlain, Hazelton, Becker, and Boyd.[1] Most of the signers affixed their names on August 2, 1776, but some signed later. Not all who voted for the Declaration on July 4, 1776, were signers; while some whose signatures appear were not in Congress when it was adopted.

Thus was given to the world a vital document which has never lost its meaning for this nation, and indeed for all humanity. Its author, Thomas Jefferson, expressed in authentic accents "the general voice of America."[2] He "gathered up the thoughts and emotions and even the characteristic phrases of the people for whom he wrote, and these he perfectly incorporated with what was already in his own mind, and then to the music of his own keen, rich, passionate and enkindling style, he mustered them into that stately and triumphant procession wherein, as some of us still think, they will go marching on to the world's end."[3]

[1] Jefferson, *Papers*, I, 299–308.

[2] *Works*, I, 22.

[3] Tyler, *The Literary History of the American Revolution*, I, 508.

The Dunlap Broadside of the Declaration of Independence

In CONGRESS, July 4, 1776.

A DECLARATION

By the REPRESENTATIVES of the
UNITED STATES OF AMERICA,
In GENERAL CONGRESS assembled.

WHEN in the Course of human Events, it becomes necessary for one People to dissolve the Political Bands which have connected them with another, and to assume among the Powers of the Earth, the separate and equal Station to which the Laws of Nature and of Nature's God entitle them, a decent Respect to the Opinions of Mankind requires that they should declare the causes which impel them to the Separation.

We hold these Truths to be self-evident, that all Men are created equal, that they are endowed by their Creator with certain unalienable Rights, that among these are Life, Liberty, and the Pursuit of Happiness—That to secure these Rights, Governments are instituted among Men, deriving their just Powers from the Consent of the Governed, that whenever any Form of Government becomes destructive of these Ends, it is the Right of the People to alter or to abolish it, and to institute new Government, laying its Foundation on such Principles, and organizing its Powers in such Form, as to them shall seem most likely to effect their Safety and Happiness. Prudence, indeed, will dictate that Governments long established should not be changed for light and transient Causes; and accordingly all Experience hath shewn, that Mankind are more disposed to suffer, while Evils are sufferable, than to right themselves by abolishing the Forms to which they are accustomed. But when a long Train of Abuses and Usurpations, pursuing invariably the same Object, evinces a Design to reduce them under absolute Despotism, it is their Right, it is their Duty, to throw off such Government, and to provide new Guards for their future Security. Such has been the patient Sufferance of these Colonies; and such is now the Necessity which constrains them to alter their former Systems of Government. The History of the present King of Great-Britain is a History of repeated Injuries and Usurpations, all having in direct Object the Establishment of an absolute Tyranny over these States. To prove this, let Facts be submitted to a candid World.

HE has refused his Assent to Laws, the most wholesome and necessary for the public Good.

HE has forbidden his Governors to pass Laws of immediate and pressing Importance, unless suspended in their Operation till his Assent should be obtained; and when so suspended, he has utterly neglected to attend to them.

HE has refused to pass other Laws for the Accommodation of large Districts of People, unless those People would relinquish the Right of Representation in the Legislature, a Right inestimable to them, and formidable to Tyrants only.

HE has called together Legislative Bodies at Places unusual, uncomfortable, and distant from the Depository of their public Records, for the sole Purpose of fatiguing them into Compliance with his Measures.

HE has dissolved Representative Houses repeatedly, for opposing with manly Firmness his Invasions on the Rights of the People.

HE has refused for a long Time, after such Dissolutions, to cause others to be elected; whereby the Legislative Powers, incapable of Annihilation, have returned to the People at large for their exercise; the State remaining in the mean time exposed to all the Dangers of Invasion from without, and Convulsions within.

HE has endeavoured to prevent the Population of these

158

States; for that Purpose obstructing the Laws for Naturalization of Foreigners; refusing to pass others to encourage their Migrations hither, and raising the Conditions of new Appropriations of Lands.

HE has obstructed the Administration of Justice, by refusing his Assent to Laws for establishing Judiciary Powers.

HE has made Judges dependent on his Will alone, for the Tenure of their Offices, and the Amount and Payment of their Salaries.

HE has erected a Multitude of new Offices, and sent hither Swarms of Officers to harrass our People, and eat out their Substance.

HE has kept among us, in Times of Peace, Standing Armies, without the consent of our Legislatures.

HE has affected to render the Military independent of and superior to the Civil Power.

HE has combined with others to subject us to a Jurisdiction foreign to our Constitution, and unacknowledged by our Laws; giving his Assent to their Acts of pretended Legislation:

FOR quartering large Bodies of Armed Troops among us:

FOR protecting them, by a mock Trial, from Punishment for any Murders which they should commit on the Inhabitants of these States:

FOR cutting off our Trade with all Parts of the World:

FOR imposing Taxes on us without our Consent:

FOR depriving us, in many Cases, of the Benefits of Trial by Jury:

FOR transporting us beyond Seas to be tried for pretended Offences:

FOR abolishing the free System of English Laws in a neighbouring Province, establishing therein an arbitrary Government, and enlarging its Boundaries, so as to render it at once an Example and fit Instrument for introducing the same absolute Rule into these Colonies:

FOR taking away our Charters, abolishing our most valuable

Laws, and altering fundamentally the Forms of our Governments:

For suspending our own Legislatures, and declaring themselves invested with Power to legislate for us in all Cases whatsoever.

He has abdicated Government here, by declaring us out of his Protection and waging War against us.

He has plundered our Seas, ravaged our Coasts, burnt our Towns, and destroyed the Lives of our People.

He is, at this Time, transporting large Armies of foreign Mercenaries to compleat the Works of Death, Desolation, and Tyranny, already begun with circumstances of Cruelty and Perfidy, scarcely paralleled in the most barbarous Ages, and totally unworthy the Head of a civilized Nation.

He has constrained our fellow Citizens taken Captive on the high Seas to bear Arms against their Country, to become the Executioners of their Friends and Brethren, or to fall themselves by their Hands.

He has excited domestic Insurrections amongst us, and has endeavoured to bring on the Inhabitants of our Frontiers, the merciless Indian Savages, whose known Rule of Warfare, is an undistinguished Destruction, of all Ages, Sexes and Conditions.

In every stage of these Oppressions we have Petitioned for Redress in the most humble Terms: Our repeated Petitions have been answered only by repeated Injury. A Prince, whose Character is thus marked by every act which may define a Tyrant, is unfit to be the Ruler of a free People.

Nor have we been wanting in Attentions to our British Brethren. We have warned them from Time to Time of Attempts by their Legislature to extend an unwarrantable Jurisdiction over us. We have reminded them of the Circumstances of our Emigration and Settlement here. We have appealed to their native Justice and Magnanimity, and we have conjured them by the Ties of our common Kindred to disavow these Usurpations, which, would inevitably interrupt our Connections and Correspondence.

They too have been deaf to the Voice of Justice and of Consanguinity. We must, therefore, acquiesce in the Necessity, which denounces our Separation, and hold them, as we hold the rest of Mankind, Enemies in War, in Peace, Friends.

We, therefore, the Representatives of the UNITED STATES OF AMERICA, in GENERAL CONGRESS, Assembled, appealing to the Supreme Judge of the World for the Rectitude of our Intentions, do, in the Name, and by Authority of the good People of these Colonies, solemnly Publish and Declare, That these United Colonies are, and of Right ought to be, FREE AND INDEPENDENT STATES; that they are absolved from all Allegiance to the British Crown, and that all political Connection between them and the State of Great-Britain, is and ought to be totally dissolved; and that as FREE AND INDEPENDENT STATES, they have full Power to levy War, conclude Peace, contract Alliances, establish Commerce, and to do all other Acts and Things which INDEPENDENT STATES may of right do. And for the support of this Declaration, with a firm Reliance on the Protection of divine Providence, we mutually pledge to each other our Lives, our Fortunes, and our sacred Honor.

Signed by ORDER *and in* BEHALF *of the* CONGRESS,

JOHN HANCOCK, PRESIDENT.

ATTEST.

CHARLES THOMSON, SECRETARY.

PHILADELPHIA: PRINTED BY JOHN DUNLAP.

Jefferson's Preamble to Virginia Constitution or Form of Government

Adopted June 29, 1776.

(Hening, *Statutes at Large*, IX, 112–13)

WHEREAS *George* the third, king of *Great Britain* and *Ireland*, and elector of *Hanover*, heretofore intrusted with the exercise of the kingly office in this government, hath endeavoured to pervert the same into a detestable and insupportable tyranny,

By putting his negative on laws the most wholesome and necessary for the publick good:

By denying his governours permission to pass laws of immediate and pressing importance, unless suspended in their operation for his assent, and, when so suspended, neglecting to attend to them for many years:

By refusing to pass certain other laws, unless the persons to be benefitted by them would relinquish the inestimable right of representation in the legislature:

By dissolving legislative Assemblies repeatedly and continually, for opposing with manly firmness his invasions of the rights of the people:

When dissolved, by refusing to call others for a long space of time, thereby leaving the political system without any legislative head:

By endeavouring to prevent the population of our country, and, for that purpose, obstructing the laws for the naturalization of foreigners:

By keeping among us, in times of peace, standing armies and ships of war:

By affecting to render the military independent of, and superiour to, the civil power:

By combining with others to subject us to a foreign jurisdiction, giving his assent to their pretended acts of legislation:

For quartering large bodies of armed troops among us:

For cutting off our trade with all parts of the world:

For imposing taxes on us without our consent:

For depriving us of the benefits of trial by jury:

For transporting us beyond seas, to be tried for pretended offences:

For suspending our own legislatures, and declaring themselves invested with power to legislate for us in all cases whatsoever:

By plundering our seas, ravaging our coasts, burning our towns, and destroying the lives of our people:

By inciting insurrections of our fellow subjects, with the allurements of forfeiture and confiscation:

By prompting our negroes to rise in arms among us, those very negroes whom, by an inhuman use of his negative, he hath refused us permission to exclude by law:

By endeavouring to bring on the inhabitants of our frontiers the merciless *Indian* savages, whose known rule of warfare is an undistinguished destruction of all ages, sexes, and conditions of existence:

By transporting, at this time, a large army of foreign mercenaries, to complete the works of death, desolation, and tyranny, already begun with circumstances of cruelty and perfidy unworthy the head of a civilized nation:

By answering our repeated petitions for redress with a repetition of injuries:

And finally, by abandoning the helm of government, and declaring us out of his allegiance and protection.

By which several acts of misrule, the government of this country, as formerly exercised under the crown of *Great Britain,* is TOTALLY DISSOLVED.

English Bill of Rights

The declaration of rights presented by the Lords and Commons to William and Mary on February 13, 1689, was formally enacted into law on December 16, 1689.

(1 Wm. and Mary, 2nd sess., c. 2. See also *Journals of the House of Commons*, X, 28–29; *Journals of the House of Lords*, XIV, 373.)

WHEREAS the late King *James* the Second, by the assistance of divers evil counsellors, judges, and ministers employed by him, did endeavour to subvert and extirpate the protestant religion, and the laws and liberties of this kingdom.

1. By assuming and exercising a power of dispensing with and suspending of laws, and the execution of laws, without consent of parliament.

2. By committing and prosecuting divers worthy prelates, for humbly petitioning to be excused from concurring to the said assumed power.

3. By issuing and causing to be executed a commission under the great seal for erecting a court called, *The court of commissioners for ecclesiastical causes.*

4. By levying money for and to the use of the crown, by pretence of prerogative, for other time, and in other manner, than the same was granted by parliament.

5. By raising and keeping a standing army within this kingdom in time of peace, without consent of parliament, and quartering soldiers contrary to law.

6. By causing several good subjects, being protestants, to be disarmed, at the same time when papists were both armed and employed, contrary to law.

7. By violating the freedom of election of members to serve in parliament.

8. By prosecutions in the court of King's bench, for matters and causes cognizable only in parliament; and by divers other arbitrary and illegal courses.

9. And whereas of late years, partial, corrupt, and unqualified persons have been returned and served on juries in trials, and particularly divers jurors in trials for high treason, which were not freeholders.

10. And excessive bail hath been required of persons committed in criminal cases, to elude the benefit of the laws made for the liberty of the subjects.

11. And excessive fines have been imposed; and illegal and cruel punishments have been inflicted.

12. And several grants and promises made of fines and forfeitures, before any conviction or judgment against the persons, upon whom the same were to be levied.

All which are utterly and directly contrary to the known laws and statutes, and freedom of this realm.

And whereas the said late king *James* the Second having abdicated the government, and the throne being thereby vacant . . . the said lords spiritual and temporal, and commons . . . do in the first place (as their ancestors in like case have usually done) for the vindicating and asserting their ancient rights and liberties, declare;

1. That the pretended power of suspending of laws, or the execution of laws, by regal authority, without consent of parliament, is illegal.

2. That the pretended power of dispensing with laws, or the execution of laws, by regal authority, as it hath been assumed and exercised of late, is illegal.

3. That the commission for erecting the late court of commissioners for ecclesiastical causes, and all other commissions and courts of like nature are illegal and pernicious.

4. That levying money for or to the use of the crown, by pretence of prerogative, without grant of parliament, for longer time, or in other manner than the same is or shall be granted, is illegal.

5. That it is the right of the subjects to petition the King, and all committments [*sic*] and prosecutions for such petitioning are illegal.

6. That the raising or keeping a standing army within the kingdom in time of peace, unless it be with consent of parliament, is against law.

7. That the subjects which are protestants, may have arms for their defence suitable to their conditions, and as allowed by law.

8. That election of members of parliament ought to be free.

9. That the freedom of speech, and debates or proceedings in parliament, ought not to be impeached or questioned in any court or place out of parliament.

10. That excessive bail ought not to be required, nor excessive fines imposed; nor cruel and unusual punishments inflicted.

11. That jurors ought to be duly impanelled and returned, and jurors which pass upon men in trials for high treason ought to be freeholders.

12. That all grants and promises of fines and forfeitures of particular persons before conviction, are illegal and void.

13. And that for redress of all grievances, and for the amending, strengthening, and preserving of the laws, parliaments ought to be held frequently.

And they do claim, demand, and insist upon all and singular the premisses, as their undoubted rights and liberties; and that no declarations, judgments, doings or proceedings, to the prejudice of the people in any of the said premisses, ought in any wise to be drawn hereafter into consequence or example.

[The Lords and Commons then went on, in their declaration, to express confidence in the Prince of Orange as protector of these rights; resolved that William and Mary be declared king and queen for life; and proposed new oaths to be taken in lieu of the oaths of allegiance and supremacy theretofore used.

After a recital of this declaration in full, and a recital of the acceptance of the crown by the Prince and Princess of Orange "according to the resolution and desire of the said lords and commons contained in the said declaration," the act of December 16, 1689, contained, among other things, the following provisions:]

VI. Now in pursuance of the premisses, the said lords spiritual and temporal, and commons, in parliament assembled, for the ratifying, confirming and establishing the said declaration, and the articles, clauses, matters, and things therein contained, by the force of a law made in due form by authority of parliament, do pray that it may be declared and enacted, That all and singular the rights and liberties asserted and claimed in the said declaration, are the true, ancient, and indubitable rights and liberties of the people of this kingdom, and so shall be esteemed, allowed, adjudged, deemed, and taken to be, and that all and every the particulars aforesaid shall be firmly and strictly holden and observed, as they are expressed in the said declaration; and all officers and ministers whatsoever shall serve their Majesties and their successors according to the same in all times to come.

XI. All which their Majesties are contented and pleased shall be declared, enacted, and established by authority of this present parliament, and shall stand, remain, and be the law of this realm for ever; and the same are by their said Majesties, by and with the advice and consent of the lords spiritual and temporal, and commons, in parliament assembled, and by the authority of the same, declared, enacted, and established accordingly.

Virginia Bill of Rights

Adopted June 12, 1776.

(*Proceedings* of the Convention, 100–103;
Hening, *Statutes at Large*, IX, 109–12)

A DECLARATION OF RIGHTS *made by the representatives of the good people of Virginia, assembled in full and free Convention; which rights do pertain to them, and their posterity, as the basis and foundation of government.*

1. THAT all men are by nature equally free and independent, and have certain inherent rights, of which, when they enter into a state of society, they cannot, by any compact, deprive or divest their posterity; namely, the enjoyment of life and liberty, with the means of acquiring and possessing property, and pursuing and obtaining happiness and safety.

2. That all power is vested in, and consequently derived from, the people; that magistrates are their trustees and servants, and at all times amenable to them.

3. That government is, or ought to be, instituted for the common benefit, protection, and security, of the people, nation, or community; of all the various modes and forms of government that is best, which is capable of producing the greatest degree of happiness and safety, and is most effectually secured against the danger of mal-administration; and that whenever any government shall be found inadequate or contrary to these purposes, a majority of the community hath an indubitable, unalienable, and indefeasible right, to reform, alter, or abolish it, in such manner as shall be judged most conducive to the publick weal.

4. That no man, or set of men, are entitled to exclusive or separate emoluments or privileges from the community, but in consideration of publick services; which, not being descendible, neither ought the offices of magistrate, legislator, or judge, to be hereditary.

5. That the legislative and executive powers of the state should be separate and distinct from the judicative; and that the members of the two first may be restrained from oppression, by feeling and

participating the burthens of the people, they should, at fixed periods, be reduced to a private station, return into that body from which they were originally taken, and the vacancies be supplied by frequent, certain, and regular elections, in which all, or any part of the former members, to be again eligible, or ineligible, as the laws shall direct.

6. That elections of members to serve as representatives of the people, in assembly, ought to be free; and that all men, having sufficient evidence of permanent common interest with, and attachment to, the community, have the right of suffrage, and cannot be taxed or deprived of their property for publick uses without their own consent, or that of their representatives so elected, nor bound by any law to which they have not, in like manner, assented, for the publick good.

7. That all power of suspending laws, or the execution of laws, by any authority without consent of the representatives of the people, is injurious to their rights, and ought not to be exercised.

8. That in all capital or criminal prosecutions a man hath a right to demand the cause and nature of his accusation, to be confronted with the accusers and witnesses, to call for evidence in his favour, and to a speedy trial by an impartial jury of his vicinage, without whose unanimous consent he cannot be found guilty, nor can he be compelled to give evidence against himself; that no man be deprived of his liberty except by the law of the land, or the judgment of his peers.

9. That excessive bail ought not to be required, nor excessive fines imposed, nor cruel and unusual punishments inflicted.

10. That general warrants, whereby any officer or messenger may be commanded to search suspected places without evidence of a fact committed, or to seize any person or persons not named, or whose offence is not particularly described and supported by evidence, are grievous and oppressive, and ought not to be granted.

11. That in controversies respecting property, and in suits between man and man, the ancient trial by jury is preferable to any other, and ought to be held sacred.

12. That the freedom of the press is one of the great bulwarks of liberty, and can never be restrained but by despotick governments.

13. That a well regulated militia, composed of the body of the people, trained to arms, is the proper, natural, and safe defence of a free state; that standing armies, in time of peace, should be avoided, as dangerous to liberty; and that, in all cases, the military should be under strict subordination to, and governed by, the civil power.

14. That the people have a right to uniform government; and therefore, that no government separate from, or independent of, the government of *Virginia*, ought to be erected or established within the limits thereof.

15. That no free government, or the blessing of liberty, can be preserved to any people but by a firm adherence to justice, moderation, temperance, frugality, and virtue, and by frequent recurrence to fundamental principles.

16. That religion, or the duty which we owe to our CREATOR, and the manner of discharging it, can be directed only by reason and conviction, not by force or violence; and therefore all men are equally entitled to the free exercise of religion, according to the dictates of conscience; and that it is the mutual duty of all to practice Christian forbearance, love, and charity, towards each other.

Bibliography

PUBLIC RECORDS
Acts of Parliament

Pickering, Danby (ed). *The Statutes at Large.* 46 vols. Cambridge, England, 1762–1807.

I have used this edition of the English statutes, following the customary practice of citing them by regnal years and chapter instead of by volume and page. The acts of Parliament in the reign of George III which aroused opposition in America are found in Volumes 26 through 31.

Most prominent of these obnoxious acts of Parliament was the Stamp Act of March 22, 1765, 5 George III, c. 12. This was repealed by the act of March 18, 1766, 6 Geo. III, c. 11. At the same time Parliament passed the Declaratory Act, 6 Geo. III, c. 12.

The five so-called "Intolerable Acts" of 1774 were the Boston Port Act of March 31, 1774, 14 Geo. III, c. 19; the Administration of Justice Act of May 20, 1774, 14 Geo. III, c. 39; the Massachusetts Government Act of May 20, 1774, 14 Geo. III, c. 45; the Quartering Act of June 2, 1774, 14 Geo. III, c. 54; and the Quebec Act of June 22, 1774, 14 Geo. III, c. 83.

Other acts of Parliament enumerated by the Continental Congress in its resolutions of October 14, 1774, as being violations of American rights were 4 Geo. III, c. 15 (Sugar Act of April 5, 1764, imposing certain duties and entrusting enforcement of acts of trade and revenue to admiralty and vice-admiralty courts); 4 Geo. III, c. 34, (prohibiting paper money and bills of credit); 5 Geo. III, c. 25 (relating to the post office); 6 Geo. III, c. 52 (repealing Sugar Act of 1764, except for duties on tea, and imposing certain other duties); 7 Geo. III, c. 41 (creating resident commissioners of customs in the Colonies); 7 Geo. III, c. 46 (Townshend Act of June 29, 1767, imposing duties on lead, glass, paper, and other articles, for revenue); 8 Geo. III, c. 22 (increasing number of vice-admiralty courts having jurisdiction of offenses against laws of trade and revenue); 12 Geo. III, c. 24 (providing for trial in England of persons burning the king's ships, dockyards, and materials of war).

Other quartering acts, besides that of June 2, 1774 (14 Geo. III, c. 54), included 5 Geo. III, c. 7; 5 Geo. III, c. 33; 6 Geo. III, c. 8; 6 Geo. III, c. 18; 7 Geo. III, c. 55. For failure to comply fully with these provisions the New York Legislature was suspended by the act of 7 Geo. III, c. 59.

The Townshend Act of June 29, 1767, 7 Geo. III, c. 46, was repealed by the act of April 12, 1770, 10 Geo. III, c. 17. A drawback on tea exported to the Colonies was provided in the act of July 2, 1767, 7 Geo. III, c. 56. Townshend accompanied his revenue act with laws strengthening enforcement by extending the jurisdiction of admiralty courts (8 Geo. III, c. 22) and providing for customs commissioners in America (7 Geo. III, c. 41).

Stamp Act Congress

For the proceedings and resolutions of the Stamp Act Congress:
Niles, Hezekiah. *Principles and Acts of the Revolution*. Baltimore, 1822.

At pages 451–61 are reprinted the documents first published in *The Weekly Register*, Vol. II, No. 47 (July 25, 1812), 337–42; *ibid.*, No. 48 (August 1, 1812), 353–55. The resolutions of October 19, 1765 appear at page 457.

Continental Congress

For the actions of this body from 1774 through 1776:
Ford, Worthington C. (ed.). *Journals of the Continental Congress*. Vols. I-V. Washington, 1904–1906.

Regarding adoption and signing of the Declaration:
Journals of Congress. Containing the Proceedings In the Year, 1776. Vol. II. Philadelphia, 1777. (See pages 241–47. At page 245 appears the statement "The foregoing declaration was by order of Congress engrossed and signed by the following members," which gave rise to the erroneous belief that the Declaration of Independence was signed on July 4.)
Secret Journals of the Acts and Proceedings of Congress. 4 vols. Boston, 1821. (See I, 18–19. The entries for July 19 and August 2, 1776, were first published here.)
See also the *Works* of Jefferson and Adams, as well as Richard Smith's Diary.

Reports of the Supreme Court of the United States, 1796–1948.
Reports of the Supreme Judicial Court of Massachusetts, 1892.
Reports of the Virginia Court of Appeals, 1806.
Laws of the United States are cited from the official *Statutes at Large.*

Other statutes are cited from the following collections:

Georgia:
Acts Passed by the General Assembly of Georgia, At a Session begun and holden at Savannah, on Thursday the 24th Day of October, Anno Domini 1765 . . . . Savannah, [1766?]. [Facsimile. Washington, 1906.]

Massachusetts:
Acts and Laws, Passed by the Great and General Court or Assembly Of the Province of the Massachusetts-Bay in New-England, From 1692, to 1719. London, 1724.
The Acts and Resolves, Public and Private, of the Province of Massachusetts Bay. Vol. III. Boston, 1878.

New Hampshire:
Acts and Laws of His Majesty's Province of New-Hampshire. Portsmouth, N. H., 1771.

New Jersey:
Acts of the General Assembly of the Province of New Jersey . . . . [April 17, 1702–January 14, 1776; edited by Samuel Allinson.] Burlington, N. J., 1776.

New York:
The Colonial Laws of New York from the Year 1664 to the Revolution. Vols. IV and V. Albany, 1894.

Pennsylvania:
The Statutes at Large of Pennsylvania from 1682 to 1801. Vols. II–XVI [no Vol. I issued]. [Harrisburg], 1896–1911.

South Carolina:
Acts Passed by the General Assembly of the Province of South-Carolina, At a Sessions [sic] begun . . . [January 19, 1747/8]. Charles-Town, 1749.
Acts of the General Assembly of South-Carolina. Passed the 12th of April 1768. Charles-Town, 1768.

Cooper, Thomas (ed.). *The Statutes at Large of South Carolina.* 5 vols. Columbia, S. C., 1836–39.

Virginia:

The Acts of Assembly, Now in Force, in the Colony of Virginia. Publish'd pursuant to an Order of the General Assembly. Williamsburg, 1752.

Acts of Assembly, Now in Force, in Virginia. Occasioned by the Repeal of Sundry Acts Made in the Twenty Second Year of His Majesty's Reign, and in the Year of Our Lord 1748. Williamsburg, 1753.

The Acts of Assembly, Now in Force, in the Colony of Virginia, With an Exact Table to the Whole. Published by Order of the General Assembly. Williamsburg, 1769.

Hening, William W. (ed.). *The Statutes at Large.* 13 vols. Richmond and Philadelphia, 1809–23.

Laws restricting slave trade:

The statement that disallowed laws to restrict the importation of slaves were passed by South Carolina in 1760, New Jersey in 1763, and Virginia in 1772 (Friedenwald, *The Declaration of Independence,* 215; Fisher, "The Twenty-Eight Charges against the King in the Declaration of Independence," *Pennsylvania Magazine of History and Biography,* Vol. XXXI, No. 3 [July, 1907], 264), I have not been able to verify from the published *Acts of the Privy Council* except in the case of Virginia. The same is true of the statement in Grahame, *History of the United States of North America,* IV, 79, that in 1761 South Carolina passed an act imposing a duty so high as to be almost prohibitory, but "this law was rescinded by the crown, as inconsistent with the interests of British commerce."

On five occasions Virginia acts were disallowed which imposed duties on the slave trade. The act of June 20, 1723 (Hening, *The Statutes at Large,* IV, 118) was disallowed by the king in council on April 30, 1724; the act of March 30, 1728 (*ibid.,* 182) on August 18, 1729; the act of April 11, 1767 (*ibid.,* VIII, 237) on August 12, 1768; two acts of December 21, 1769 (*ibid.,* 337, 342) on December 9, 1770; and the act of April 11, 1772 (*ibid.,* 530) on April 7, 1773. *Acts of the Privy Council,* III, 64–65; V, 164–65, 286–88, 362–63. Moreover, it seems that a Pennsylvania act of February 26,

1773, was disallowed on July 6, 1774. *Ibid.*, V, 398. Cf. *Statutes at Large of Pennsylvania*, VIII, 332.

A New Jersey act of September 25, 1762 (chap. 369) apparently "was not laid before the King by the Lords of Trade, for certain Reasons which were obviated in a future Law [chap. 494]." *Acts of the General Assembly of the Province of New Jersey*, 253. This may perhaps be regarded as the political equivalent of disallowance. No other instance is given in the table of acts disallowed or obsolete in Allinson's compilation of New Jersey laws. In South Carolina the acts of April 5, 1740, and August 25, 1764 (Cooper, *The Statutes at Large of South Carolina*, III, 556; IV, 187), apparently took effect without any hindrance by the king in council. Donnan, *Documents*, IV, 297, 301, 401. No disallowance of any New Jersey or South Carolina acts against the slave trade is indicated in the volumes of *Acts of the Privy Council* which cover the period 1745–83.

Other State Papers

Acts of the Privy Council of England. Colonial Series. 6 vols. London, 1908–12. (Vol. V covers the period 1766–83.)

Alien and Sedition Laws. 62 Cong., 2 sess., *Sen. Doc. 873.* Washington, 1912.

Almon, John. *A Collection of Interesting and Authentic Papers, relative to the Dispute between Great Britain and America; Shewing the Causes and Progress of that Misunderstanding, from 1764 to 1775.* London, 1777. Cited as Almon, *Prior Documents.*

Bouton, Nathaniel (ed.). *Provincial Papers. Documents and Records relating to the Province of New-Hampshire.* 7 vols. Concord, [Manchester, and Nashua], 1867–73.

The Colonial Records of North Carolina. Vols. V–IX. Raleigh, N. C., 1887–90.

Documents Relating to the Colonial History of the State of New Jersey. Vol. IX. Newark, N. J., 1885.

Documents Relative to the Colonial History of the State of New-York. Vols. VI–VIII. Albany, N. Y., 1855–57.

Force, Peter. *American Archives.* 4th series. Vols. I–VI. Washington, 1837–46.

Massachusetts State Papers. [Alden Bradford, ed.] *Speeches of the Governors of Massachusetts, from 1765 to 1775; and the An-*

swers of the House of Representatives to the same; with their Resolutions and Addresses for that Period. And other Public Papers relating to the Dispute between this Country and Great Britain, which Led to the Independence of the United States. Boston, 1818. Cited as *Massachusetts State Papers*.

"Instructions to Lord Dunmore" [February 11, 1771], in *Aspinwall Papers*. Part II. *Collections of the Massachusetts Historical Society* (4th series). Boston, 1871. Pages 630–66.

Journals of the House of Burgesses of Virginia, 1752–76. Edited by Henry R. McIlwaine and John P. Kennedy. Richmond, 1905–1909.

The Proceedings of the Convention of Delegates For the Counties and Corporations In the Colony of Virginia, Held at Richmond Town, in the County of Henrico, On the 20th of March 1775. Williamsburg, [1775].

The Proceedings of the Convention of Delegates, Held at the Capitol, in the City of Williamsburg, in the Colony of Virginia, on Monday the 6th of May, 1776. Williamsburg, [1776].

CONTEMPORARY PAMPHLETS

Among the pamphlets expressing the English position in the dispute with America may be mentioned:

[Chandler, Thomas B.] *A Friendly Address to All Reasonable Americans, on The Subject of Our Political Confusions: In Which the Necessary Consequences of Violently Opposing the King's Troops, and of a General Non-Importation Are Fairly Stated.* New York, 1774.

Johnson, Samuel. *Taxation no Tyranny.* London, 1775. (A forceful polemic by Boswell's hero.)

[Knox, William.] *The Controversy between Great Britain and her Colonies Reviewed.* London, 1769. (A good statement of the English position. Contains Stamp Act resolutions of four colonies as well as the Congress.)

Macpherson, James. *The Rights of Great Britain Asserted Against the Claims of America: Being an Answer to the Declaration of the General Congress.* London, 1776. (A reply to the *Declaration on Taking up Arms* by the author of Ossian's poems.)

The Supremacy of the British Legislature over the Colonies Candidly Discussed. London, 1775.

The American attitude was set forth in the following writings:

An Argument in Defence of the Exclusive Right Claimed by the Colonies to Tax Themselves, with a Review of the Laws of England Relative to Representation and Taxation. London, 1774.

Bland, Richard. *An Inquiry into the Rights of the British Colonies.* Williamsburg, 1766.

Burgh, James. *Political Disquisitions.* 3 vols. Philadelphia, 1775.

Dulany, Daniel. *Considerations on the Propriety of Imposing Taxes in the British Colonies, For the Purpose of raising a Revenue, by act of Parliament.* Boston, 1766 [?].

Franklin, Benjamin. *The Causes of the Present Distractions in America Explained: In Two Letters to a Merchant in London.* Boston [?], 1774.

Otis, James. *Some Political Writings of James Otis.* Edited by Charles F. Mullett. Columbia, Mo., 1929.

[Paine, Thomas.] *Common Sense; Addressed to the Inhabitants of America.* Philadelphia, 1776.

Price, Richard. *Observations on the Nature of Civil Liberty, the Principles of Government, and the Justice and Policy of the War with America.* London, 1776.

Priestley, Joseph. *An Address to Protestant Dissenters of All Denominations, On the Approaching Election of Members of Parliament, With Respect to the State of Public Liberty in General, and of American Affairs in Particular.* London, 1774.

——. *An Essay on the First Principles of Government, and on the Nature of Political, Civil and Religious Liberty.* 2nd edition. London, 1771.

See also Jefferson's *Summary View*, Dickinson's *Essay*, and James Wilson's *Considerations*, all published in 1774.

ARTICLES

Abbott, Everett V. "Inalienable Rights and the Eighteenth Amendment," *Columbia Law Review*, Vol. XX, No. 2 (February, 1920), 183–95.

Andrews, Charles M. "The Royal Disallowance," *Proceedings of the*

American Antiquarian Society, Vol. XXIV (new series), Part 2 (October, 1914), 342–62.

Barnhart, Arthur M. "Princeton and the Problems of a Democracy," *Nassau Literary Magazine,* Vol. LXXIX (April, 1924), 361–70.

Boyd, Julian P. "New Light on Jefferson and His Great Task," *The New York Times Magazine,* April 13, 1947, p. 17 ff.

Burnett, Edmund C. "The Name 'United States of America,'" *American Historical Review,* Vol. XXXI, No. 1 (October, 1925), 79–81.

Carpenter, A. H. "Naturalization in England and the American Colonies," *American Historical Review,* Vol. IX, No. 2 (January, 1904), 288–303.

Chamberlain, Mellen. "The Authentication of the Declaration of Independence, July 4, 1776," *Proceedings of the Massachusetts Historical Society* (2nd series), Vol. I (November, 1884), 273–98.

Corwin, Edward S. "The 'Higher Law' Background of American Constitutional Law," *Harvard Law Review,* Vol. XLII, No. 2 (December, 1928), 149–85; *ibid.,* No. 3, (January, 1929), 365–409.

Dana, William F. "The Declaration of Independence," *Harvard Law Review,* Vol. XIII, No. 5 (January, 1900), 319–43.

Dumbauld, Edward. "Dissenting Opinions in International Adjudication," *University of Pennsylvania Law Review,* Vol. XC, No. 8 (June, 1942), 929–45.

———. "Jefferson and Local Government," *The County Officer,* Vol. XV, No. 1 (April, 1950), 8–10, 28–29.

———. "The Place of Philosophy in International Law," *University of Pennsylvania Law Review,* Vol. LXXXIII, No. 5 (March, 1935), 590–606.

———. "Valedictory Opinions of Mr. Justice Holmes," *Michigan Law Review,* Vol. XLII, No. 6 (June, 1944), 1037–48.

Fenwick, Charles G. "The Authority of Vattel," *American Political Science Review,* Vol. VII, No. 3 (August, 1913), 395–410.

Fisher, Sydney G. "The Twenty-Eight Charges against the King in the Declaration of Independence," *Pennsylvania Magazine of History and Biography,* Vol. XXXI, No. 3 (July, 1907), 257–303.

Friedenwald, Herbert. "The Declaration of Independence," *The International Monthly*, Vol. IV, No. 1 (July, 1901), 102–21.

Ganter, Herbert L. "Jefferson's 'Pursuit of Happiness' and Some Forgotten Men," *The William and Mary Quarterly* (2nd series), Vol. XVI, No. 3 (July, 1936), 422–34; *ibid.*, No. 4 (October, 1936), 558–88.

Hays, Isaac Minis. "A Note on the History of the Jefferson Manuscript Draught of the Declaration of Independence in the Library of the American Philosophical Society," *Proceedings of the American Philosophical Society*, Vol. XXXVII, No. 1 (July, 1898), 88–107.

Jackson, Robert H. Address, April 13, 1945, in *Proceedings of the Washington Meeting of the American Society of International Law* (1945).

Koch, Adrienne, and Harry Ammon. "The Virginia and Kentucky Resolutions: An Episode in Jefferson's and Madison's Defense of Civil Liberties," *The William and Mary Quarterly* (3rd series), Vol. V, No. 2 (April, 1948), 145–76.

Lewis, Anthony M. "Jefferson and Virginia's Pioneers, 1774–1781," *Mississippi Valley Historical Review*, Vol. XXXIV, No. 4 (March, 1948), 551–88.

McLaughlin, Andrew C. "American History and American Democracy," *American Historical Review*, Vol. XX, No. 2 (January, 1915), 255–76.

———. "The Background of American Federalism," *American Political Science Review*, Vol. XIII, No. 2 (May, 1918), 215–40.

———. "Social Compact and Constitutional Construction," *American Historical Review*, Vol. V, No. 3 (April, 1900), 467–90.

———. "The Western Posts and the British Debts," *Annual Report of the American Historical Association for the Year 1894*, 413–44.

Martin, William H. "Some Virginia Law Books in a Virginia Law Office," *Virginia Law Register* (new series), Vol. XII, No. 6 (October, 1926), 321–30.

Morgan, Edmund S. "Colonial Ideas of Parliamentary Power 1764–1766," *The William and Mary Quarterly* (3rd series), Vol. V, No. 3 (July, 1948), 311–41.

Pollock, Sir Frederick. "The History of the Law of Nature," *Columbia Law Review*, Vol. I, No. 1 (January, 1901), 11–32; *ibid.*, Vol. II, No. 3 (March, 1902), 131–43.

Pound, Roscoe. "The End of Law as Developed in Juristic Thought," *Harvard Law Review*, Vol. XXVII, No. 1 (May, 1914), 605–28.

———. "Liberty of Contract," *Yale Law Journal*, Vol. XVIII, No. 7 (May, 1909), 454–87.

———. "The Revival of Natural Law," *Notre Dame Lawyer*, Vol. XVII, No. 4 (June, 1942), 287–372.

Radin, Max. "The Myth of Magna Carta," *Harvard Law Review*, Vol. LX, No. 7 (September, 1947), 1060–91.

Smith, Richard. "Diary of Richard Smith in the Continental Congress, 1775–1776," *American Historical Review*, Vol. I, No. 2 (April, 1896), 493–516.

Stillé, Charles J. "Pennsylvania and the Declaration of Independence," *Pennsylvania Magazine of History and Biography*, Vol. XIII, No. 4 (January, 1890), 385–429.

Stuart, Cora. "Naturalization in the English Colonies of America," *Annual Report of the American Historical Association for the Year 1893*, 319–28.

Sullivan, James. "The Antecedents of the Declaration of Independence," *Annual Report of the American Historical Association for 1902*, I, 66–85.

Van Tyne, Claude H. "Sovereignty in the American Revolution," *American Historical Review*, Vol. XII, No. 3 (April, 1907), 529–45.

Warren, Charles. "The New 'Liberty' under the Fourteenth Amendment," *Harvard Law Review*, Vol. XXXIX, No. 4 (February, 1926), 431–63.

Wilkin, Robert N. "Status of Natural Law in American Jurisprudence," *Notre Dame Lawyer*, Vol. XXIV, No. 3 (Spring, 1949), 343–63.

Wiltse, Charles M. "Thomas Jefferson on the Law of Nations," *American Journal of International Law*, Vol. XXIX, No. 1 (January, 1935), 66–81.

BOOKS

Abernethy, Thomas P. *Western Lands and the American Revolution.* Boston, 1943.

Adams, George B., and H. M. Stephens. *Select Documents of English Constitutional History.* New York, 1901.

Adams, John. *The Works of John Adams.* Edited by Charles Francis Adams. 10 vols. Boston, 1850–56.

Adams, John Quincy. *Memoirs of John Quincy Adams.* Edited by Charles Francis Adams. 12 vols. Philadelphia, 1874–77.

———. *Parties in the United States.* Edited by Charles T. Adams. New York, 1941.

Adams, Randolph G. *Political Ideas of the American Revolution.* Durham, N. C., 1922.

Allen, John W. *A History of Political Thought in the Sixteenth Century.* New York, 1928.

Allman, Norwood F. *Shanghai Lawyer.* New York, 1943.

Aquinas, Thomas. *Basic Writings of Saint Thomas Aquinas.* Edited by Anton C. Pegis. 2 vols. New York, 1945.

Aristotle. *The Nicomachean Ethics of Aristotle.* Translated by J.E.C. Welldon. London, 1897.

Barker, Ernest (ed.). *Social Contract.* Oxford, Eng., 1947.

Becker, Carl. *The Declaration of Independence.* New York, 1922.

———. *New Liberties for Old.* New Haven, 1941.

Bemis, Samuel F. *Jay's Treaty: A Study in Commerce and Diplomacy.* New York, 1923.

Bentham, Jeremy. *An Introduction to the Principles of Morals and Legislation.* Oxford, Eng., 1789.

Bland, Richard. *A Fragment on the Pistole Fee, claimed by the Governor of Virginia, 1753.* Edited by Worthington C. Ford. Brooklyn, 1891.

Bolingbroke, Henry St. John. *The Works of Lord Bolingbroke.* 4 vols. Philadelphia, 1841.

Boyd, Julian P. *The Declaration of Independence.* Washington, 1943; 2nd edition, Princeton, 1945. Citations are from 2nd edition.

Bracton. *De Legibus et Consuetudinibus Angliae.* Edited by George E. Woodbine. 4 vols. New Haven, 1915–42.

Bridgman, Percy W. *The Intelligent Individual and Society.* New York, 1938.

Brierly, James L. *The Law of Nations*. Oxford, Eng., 1928.

Brown, Samuel G. *The Life of Rufus Choate*. Boston, 1898.

Burnett, Edmund C. (ed.). *Letters of Members of the Continental Congress*. 8 vols. Washington, 1921–36.

Chalmers, George. *An Introduction to the History of the Revolt of the American Colonies*. 2 vols. Boston, 1845.

———. *Opinions of Eminent Lawyers, on Various Points of English Jurisprudence, Chiefly Concerning the Colonies, Fisheries, and Commerce, of Great Britain*. 2 vols. London, 1814.

Chinard, Gilbert. *The Literary Bible of Thomas Jefferson*. Baltimore and Paris, 1928.

———. *Thomas Jefferson, the Apostle of Americanism*. Boston, 1929.

Cicero. *The Republic of Cicero*. Edited by G. G. Hardingham. London, 1884.

Cobb, Sanford H. *The Rise of Religious Liberty in America*. New York, 1902.

Conway, Moncure D. *Omitted Chapters of History Disclosed in the Life and Papers of Edmund Randolph*. New York, 1888.

Corwin, Edward S. *Total War and the Constitution*. New York, 1947.

Crandall, Samuel B. *Treaties, Their Making and Enforcement*. 2nd edition. Washington, 1916.

Crump, Helen J. *Colonial Admiralty Jurisdiction in the Seventeenth Century*. London, 1931.

Dicey, Albert V. *Introduction to the Study of the Law of the Constitution*. 8th edition. London, 1915.

Dickinson, Edwin D. *The Equality of States in International Law*. Cambridge, Mass., 1920.

Dickinson, John. *An Essay on the Constitutional Power of Great-Britain over the Colonies in America*. Philadelphia, 1774.

———. *Letters from a Farmer in Pennsylvania, To the Inhabitants of the British Colonies*. Boston, 1768. (First published in Philadelphia in 1768.)

———. *The Political Writings of John Dickinson*. 2 vols. Wilmington, Del., 1801.

———. *The Writings of John Dickinson*. Edited by P. L. Ford. Philadelphia, 1895.

Dickinson, John. *Administrative Justice and the Supremacy of Law in the United States.* Cambridge, Mass., 1927.

Digges, Sir Dudley. *The Unlawfulness of Subjects Taking up Arms against their Soveraigne in what case soever.* London, 1662.

Donaldson, Thomas. *The House in Which Thomas Jefferson Wrote the Declaration of Independence.* Philadelphia, 1898.

Donnan, Elizabeth (ed.). *Documents Illustrative of the History of the Slave Trade to America.* 4 vols. Washington, 1930-35.

Douglass, William. *A Summary, Historical and Political, of the First Planting, Progressive Improvements, and Present State. of the British Settlements in North-America.* 2 vols. London, 1760.

Dumbauld, Edward. *Interim Measures of Protection in International Controversies.* The Hague, 1932.

————. *Thomas Jefferson, American Tourist.* Norman, 1946.

Dunning, William A. *A History of Political Thought from Luther to Montesquieu.* New York, 1905.

Etting, Frank M. *The History of Independence Hall.* Boston, 1876.

Euripides with an English Translation. Translated by Arthur S. Way. Cambridge, Mass., 1908.

Farrand, Max. *The Development of the United States from Colonies to a World Power.* Boston, 1918.

Figgis, John N. *The Divine Right of Kings.* 2nd edition. Cambridge, Eng., 1914.

Fitzpatrick, John C. *The Spirit of the Revolution.* Boston, 1924.

Friedenwald, Herbert. *The Declaration of Independence.* New York, 1904.

George, Staughton (ed.). *Compilation of the Laws and Ordinances Establishing the Several Courts of Judicature in the Province of Pennsylvania.* Harrisburg, 1879.

Gierke, Otto von. *Natural Law and the Theory of Society, 1500 to 1800.* Translated with an Introduction by Ernest Barker. Cambridge, Eng., 1934.

Giles, Herbert A. *A History of Chinese Literature.* New York, 1901.

Gooch, George P. *The History of English Democratic Ideas in the Seventeenth Century.* Cambridge, Eng., 1898.

————. *Political Thought in England from Bacon to Halifax.* London, 1914-15.

Goodrich, Charles S. *Lives of the Signers to the Declaration of Independence*. New-York, 1829.

Gough, John W. *The Social Contract*. Oxford, Eng., 1936.

Grahame, James. *The History of the United States of North America, from the Plantation of the British Colonies till their Revolt and Declaration of Independence*. 4 vols. London, 1836.

Gray, John Chipman. *The Nature and Sources of the Law*. 2nd edition. New York, 1921.

Greene, Evarts B. *The Provincial Governor in the English Colonies of North America*. New York, 1898.

Grigsby, Hugh Blair. *The Virginia Convention of 1776*. Richmond, 1855.

Grotius, Hugo. *De Jure Belli ac Pacis Libri Tres*. Vol. II. Oxford, Eng., 1925. (First published in 1625. Translated by Francis W. Kelsey from edition of 1646.)

Haines, Charles G. *The Revival of Natural Law Concepts*. Cambridge, Mass., 1930.

Hamilton, Alexander. *The Works of Alexander Hamilton*. Edited by Henry C. Lodge. 12 vols. New York, 1904.

Hazelton, John H. *The Declaration of Independence: Its History*. New York, 1906.

Hinkhouse, Fred J. *The Preliminaries of the American Revolution as Seen in the English Press 1763–1775*. New York, 1926.

Hobbes, Thomas. *Leviathan*. Edited by A. D.Lindsay. London, 1914. (First published in 1651.)

Holdsworth, William S. *A History of English Law*. Vol. XI. Boston, 1938.

Holmes, Oliver W., Jr. *Collected Legal Papers*. New York, 1920.
———. *The Common Law*. Boston, 1881.

Holst, Hermann E. von. *The Constitutional and Political History of the United States*. Vol. I. Chicago, 1877.

Hosmer, James K. *The Life of Thomas Hutchinson Royal Governor of the Province of Massachusetts Bay*. Boston, 1896.

Howe, Mark DeWolfe (ed.). *Readings in American Legal History*. Cambridge, Mass., 1949.

Hume, David. *Essays, Moral and Political*. 3rd edition. London, 1748.

Hutchinson, Peter O. (ed.). *The Diary and Letters of His Excellency Thomas Hutchinson, Esq.* 2 vols. London, 1883–86.

Hutchinson, Thomas. *The History of the Province of Massachusetts Bay, from the Year 1750, until June, 1774.* Vol. III. London, 1828.

———. *Strictures upon the Declaration of the Congress at Philadelphia, In a Letter to a Noble Lord.* London, 1776. (An explanation of the American grievances to the English by the last royal civilian governor of Massachusetts, whose acts constituted many of such grievances.)

Jefferson, Thomas. *The Papers of Thomas Jefferson.* Edited by Julian P. Boyd, Lyman H. Butterfield, and Mina R. Bryan. Vol. I. Princeton, 1950. (This indispensably valuable volume, the first fruits of a monumental and admirably executed enterprise, was received after my book was in proof form; hence I have been able to insert only a few references to it. Covering the years 1760 to 1776, it contains much useful material and extensive editorial notes regarding the Declaration of Independence and kindred documents.)

———. *Reports of Cases Determined in the General Court of Virginia. From 1730 to 1740, and from 1768 to 1772.* Charlottesville, Va., 1829.

———. *A Summary View of the Rights of British America.* Edited by Thomas P. Abernethy. New York, 1943. (First published in Williamsburg in 1774.)

———. *The Works of Thomas Jefferson.* Edited by Paul Leicester Ford. Federal edition. 12 vols. New York, 1904.

———. *The Writings of Thomas Jefferson.* Edited by Andrew A. Lipscomb and Albert E. Bergh. Memorial edition. 20 vols. Washington, 1903–1904.

Jensen, Merrill. *The Articles of Confederation.* 2nd edition. Madison, Wis., 1948.

Jessup, Philip C. *A Modern Law of Nations.* New York, 1948.

Justinian. *Corpus Juris Civilis.* Edited by Theodor Mommsen and Paul Krueger. Vol. I. 12th edition. Berlin, 1911.

Kelsen, Hans. *Allgemeine Staatslehre.* Berlin, 1925.

———. *Law and Peace in International Relations.* Cambridge, Mass., 1942.

Kimball, Marie G. *Jefferson: The Road to Glory.* New York, 1943.

Koch, Adrienne. *Jefferson and Madison.* New York, 1950.

———. *The Philosophy of Thomas Jefferson.* New York, 1943.

Labaree, Leonard W. *Royal Instructions to British Colonial Governors 1670–1776.* 2 vols. New York, 1935.

Lecky, William E. H. *The American Revolution, 1763–1783.* Edited by James A. Woodburn. New York, 1898.

Lee, Richard Henry. *Letters of Richard Henry Lee.* Edited by James C. Ballagh. 2 vols. New York, 1911–14.

Lincoln, Charles H. *The Revolutionary Movement in Pennsylvania.* Philadelphia, 1901.

[Lind, John.] *An Answer to the Declaration of the American Congress.* London, 1776. (A valuable contemporary analysis of the American grievances from the English point of view.)

Locke, John. *Two Treatises of Government.* London, 1690; edited by William S. Carpenter, London, 1924. Citations are to the 1924 edition.

McCrady, Edward. *The History of South Carolina under the Royal Government.* New York, 1899.

Macdonald, William. *Documentary Source Book of American History.* 3rd edition. New York, 1926.

McIlwain, Charles H. *The American Revolution: A Constitutional Interpretation.* New York, 1923.

McLaughlin, Andrew C. *A Constitutional History of the United States.* New York, 1935.

———. *The Foundations of American Constitutionalism.* New York, 1932.

MacLeish, Archibald. *A Time to Speak.* Boston, 1941.

McRee, Griffith J. *Life and Correspondence of James Iredell.* 2 vols. New York, 1857–58.

Madison, James. *The Writings of James Madison.* Edited by Gaillard Hunt. 9 vols. New York, 1910.

Maitland, Frederick W. *The Constitutional History of England.* Cambridge, Eng., 1908.

Malone, Dumas. *Jefferson the Virginian.* Boston, 1948.

Martin, François-Xavier. *The History of North Carolina, from the Earliest Period.* 2 vols. New-Orleans, 1829.

Michael, William H. *The Declaration of Independence.* Washington, 1904.

Miller, John C. *Origins of the American Revolution.* Boston, 1943.

Milton, John. *The Works of John Milton*. Edited by Frank A. Patterson. Vol. V. New York, 1932.

Montesquieu, Charles Louis de. *Lettres Persanes*. Edited by Henri Barckhausen. 2 vols. Paris, 1913. (First published in 1721.)

Moore, Frank. *Diary of the American Revolution. From Newspapers and Original Documents*. 2 vols. New York, 1860.

Morison, Samuel E. *Sources and Documents illustrating the American Revolution*. Oxford, Eng., 1923.

Mullett, Charles F. *Fundamental Law and the American Revolution*. New York, 1923.

The Parliamentary History of England, from the Earliest Period to the Year 1803. Vols. XVI–XVIII (1765–77). London, 1813.

Parish, John C. *The Emergence of the Idea of Manifest Destiny*. Los Angeles, 1932.

Plato. *The Dialogues of Plato*. Translated by Benjamin Jowett. Vol. II. New York, 1874.

Pollock, Sir Frederick. *Essays in the Law*. London, 1922.

Pope, Alexander. *An Essay on Man: In Four Epistles. To Henry St. John, Lord Bolingbroke*. London, 1772. (First published in 1732–34.)

Pound, Roscoe. *Law and Morals*. 2nd edition. Chapel Hill, 1926.

Pownall, Thomas. *The Administration of the British Colonies*. 6th edition. 2 vols. London, 1777. (Part I published in 1764; Part II, in 1774).

Pufendorf, Samuel. *De Jure Naturae et Gentium Libri Octo*. 2 vols. Oxford, Eng., 1934. (First published in Lund, Sweden, in 1672.)

Quincy, Samuel M. (ed.). *Reports of Cases Argued and Adjudged in the Superior Court of Judicature of the Province of Massachusetts Bay, between 1761 and 1772. By Josiah Quincy, Junior*. Boston, 1865.

Randall, Henry S. *The Life of Thomas Jefferson*. 3 vols. New York, 1858.

Redlich, Josef. *The Procedure of the House of Commons*. 3 vols. London, 1908.

Rushworth, John. *Historical Collections*. 8 vols. London, 1721–22. (First published in London, 1659–1701. The 1721–22 edition belonging to Jefferson is in the Library of Congress.)

Russell, Elmer B. *Review of American Colonial Legislation by the King in Council*. New York, 1915.

Sanderson, John. *Biography of the Signers to the Declaration of Independence*. 9 vols. Philadelphia. 1820–27.

Santayana, George. *The Middle Span*. New York, 1945.

Scott, James Brown. *Sovereign States and Suits before Arbitral Tribunals and Courts of Justice*. New York, 1925.

Selden, John. *The Table Talk of John Selden*. Edited by Samuel H. Reynolds. Oxford, Eng., 1892.

Selsam, John P. *The Pennsylvania Constitution of 1776*. Philadelphia, 1936.

Smith, William R. *South Carolina as a Royal Province*. New York, 1903.

Staples, William R. *The Documentary History of the Destruction of the Gaspee*. Providence, 1845.

Stephen, Sir James Fitzjames. *Horae Sabbaticae*. 3 vols. London, 1892.

Stillé, Charles J. *The Life and Times of John Dickinson*. Philadelphia, 1891.

Stubbs, William. *The Constitutional History of England*. 4th edition. 3 vols. Oxford, Eng., 1896.

Thomas, Charles M. *American Neutrality in 1793*. New York, 1931.

Tudor, William. *The Life of James Otis*. Boston, 1823.

Tyler, Moses C. *The Literary History of the American Revolution*. 2 vols. New York, 1897.

Van Doren, Carl. *The Great Rehearsal*. New York, 1948.

Vattel, Emmerich de. *Le Droit des Gens, ou Principes de la Loi naturelle Appliqués à la conduite & aux affaires des nations & des souverains*. 3 vols. "London," 1758. (This first edition, belonging to Jefferson, is in the Library of Congress. It was actually published in Neuchâtel.)

———. *The Law of Nations or the Principles of Natural Law Applied to the Conduct and to the Affairs of Nations and Sovereigns*. Translated by Charles G. Fenwick. Vol. III. Washington, 1916.

Warfield, Ethelbert D. *The Kentucky Resolutions of 1798*. New York, 1887.

Warren, Charles. *The Supreme Court and Sovereign States*. Princeton, 1924.

Washburne, George A. *Imperial Control of the Administration of*

Justice in the Thirteen American Colonies, 1684–1776. New York, 1923.

Washington, George. *The Writings of George Washington.* Edited by John C. Fitzpatrick. 39 vols. Washington, 1931–44.

Wells, William V. *The Life and Public Services of Samuel Adams.* 3 vols. Boston, 1865.

Williams, Sir John Fischer. *Chapters on Current International Law and the League of Nations.* London, 1929.

Williston, Samuel. *The Law of Contracts.* 5 vols. New York, 1920–22.

Wilson, James. *Considerations on the Nature and the Extent of the Legislative Authority of the British Parliament.* Philadelphia, 1774.
———. *The Works of the Honourable James Wilson.* 3 vols. Philadelphia, 1804.

Wright, Benjamin F., Jr. *American Interpretations of Natural Law.* Cambridge, Mass., 1931.

ADDITIONAL ITEMS (2d printing)

Morgan, Edmund S. and Helen M. *The Stamp Act Crisis.* Chapel Hill, 1953.

Root, Winfred T. *The Relations of Pennsylvania with the British Government 1696–1765.* New York, 1912.

Smith, Joseph H. *Appeals to the Privy Council from the American Plantations.* New York, 1950.

Walsh, Michael J. "Contemporary Broadside Editions of the Declaration of Independence," *Harvard Library Bulletin,* Vol. III, No. 1 (Winter, 1949), 31–43.

Index